"Keith went from being flat broke in a dead-end job to owning a successful 6 figure business in 2 years."
Joshua Latimer, Founder AutomateGrowSell

The Secret Formula On

How to MAKE $500 A DAY
CLEANING WINDOWS

WITH NO STARTUP MONEY

THE #1 NEW
BESTSELLER AND
YOUTUBE
PHENOMENON

THE WINDOW CLEANING
BLUEPRINT

KEITH KALFAS

The Window Cleaning Blueprint

The Window Cleaning Blueprint
How to Make $500 a Day Cleaning Windows

By Keith Kalfas

Introduction

Want to make $500 a day cleaning windows?

Whether you're looking to start a brand new window cleaning business or already own an existing business.
The Window Cleaning Blueprint is the perfect combination of a how to guide mixed with a classic struggle to victory story.
From time-management tips to pricing to
"In your face" truth about the frustrations and struggles of growing a small business from the ground up.
Keith Kalfas tells it the way it is.

PREFACE

In this book we will discover many principles on running a successful window cleaning business.
Do not skip through this book with the intentions of only wanting to learn the
how to stuff and how much to charge for cleaning windows.

That my friend, I promise, Will only lead you down a dead-end road of frustration in this business.

Yes, we will discuss in great detail, exactly how much to charge for cleaning windows in almost every possible scenario.

Yes, we will discuss how to get your hands on a water fed pole system for cheaper than you see on these window cleaning websites.

Yes, we will learn how to overcome the fears of carrying a ladder into a customer's gigantic house and charging them $500 just to clean their windows.

But, this is a mindset business. this business might even be more about mindset than a lawn care business, a plumbing business or a general small business. A professional window cleaning business owner would back me up with that statement.

Most small businesses set a price and that's a wrap. the window cleaning business is rooted almost entirely in the perception of the buyer.

51% or more of this business is rooted in perceptions and luxury. The other 49%
"in my personal opinion" is necessity.
But when it comes to Residential homes. Primarily what we'll be discussing in this book.
Window Cleaning is a luxury business.

In the more advanced stages of the business. You can acquire large commercial accounts from city buildings, nursing homes, healthcare facilities to libraries and even skyscrapers.

In my opinion, aside from those parameters and environments. Window cleaning is not an absolute necessity to average income people.

In this book I will teach you deep, valuable shortcuts to painful lessons, that I had to learn the hard way.
Because "for the life of me". I couldn't wrap my mind around the nature of this business.
Not until the day I finally woke up and realized that the window cleaning business is a luxury business.

Have some patience, and stick with me on this. if you really buckle down and commit.
There's a magic in the process.
Welcome to,

The Window Cleaning Blueprint.

My Promise to You

 If you want to start a window cleaning business. I guarantee you that this will be the best book you've ever read on this topic in your entire life.

In this book you will learn how to overcome the many obstacles that a new window cleaning business owner faces from the moment he wakes up to the moment he goes to bed.

Sure, You will learn how to make $500 a day from cleaning windows.
The first I want your full attention. listen to me clearly.

 Starting and growing a window cleaning business is simple, but it's not easy.
 the functions and modalities of passing out business cards, registering a business, selling jobs, cleaning windows and collecting money... are a piece of cake.

All that stuff is a joke in comparison to the immense amount of frustration It takes to start and grow a successful window cleaning business.

If there's any business that looks easier to start from the outside, it's the window cleaning business. And if there's any business that will make you pull your hair out in total confusion in face of the blatant obvious, my friend, it's the window cleaning business.

Join me in this exciting journey and give me the permission to be your coach as I show you how to successfully start, grow and achieve your dream of not only making some serious money, But own your very own successful window cleaning business.

In This Book You're Going to Learn

How to start an extremely profitable window cleaning business with low overhead.
Even if you're unsure
"if this thing is really going to work',
If you have no clue what to charge,
If you have no idea what to say to sell jobs
If you're afraid of investing money and losing it
If you don't know what the requirements are for getting inside of high-end homes.
If you already have plenty of competition in your city
If you have literally no startup money, "but need money now"

Stick with me and I'll walk you through step by step,

I have clients that I coach who went from flat broke to getting there window cleaning businesses off the ground and making money in less than a week.
I know quite a few guys personally who make a killing cleaning windows.
My friend Brandon here in Michigan cleans windows and installs gutter guards on huge houses and makes $1,000 a day minimum every single day.
On some weeks, if you clean a bunch of large houses and maybe a large church you can clear $10k in a single week.

I can't promise you instant results like these guys. Growing a legitimate window cleaning business with a healthy client base takes some time. But I am making a huge promise that there's definitely
money to be made cleaning window. Windows are literally everywhere.

You can do this … and make lots of money too!

Introduction

So you want to start a window cleaning business?

First, Let me define the major problem.

Starting a window cleaning business can be extremely hard and frustrating.
Not knowing what to charge, feeling overwhelmed by all the competition,
not knowing how to start, where to start, what tools to use,
questioning if you can actually even be successful at it,
how to sell and get jobs, get insurance or a hundred other questions.

I had all these questions too in the beginning.
At times I was very discouraged because no one was there to coach me or help me and I had no choice but to hit the ground running and learn the entire business myself.

So be aware.
In today's world, the way of doing business is changing very quickly.
There's a "New Way", a "New Reality".
Things are not like they used to be.
And only the latest cutting edge information technology will keep you up to date and ahead of the pack.

This is my reason for creating The Window Cleaning Blueprint. My goal in this program is to effectively guide you through the minefield and equip you with the right information and tools necessary in order to get your window cleaning business off the ground successfully....and fast!

Hi I'm Keith Kalfas and I own a successful window cleaning business.

I've cleaned windows from high profile customers in high end homes making over $2000 profit a day... to cleaning windows at cellphone stores, restaurants, gas stations, sub shops and liquor stores for literally peanuts.

I started broke and desperate and in fear with only $50 in my pocket and nothing but a small business opportunity magazine.

To making tens of thousands of dollars cleaning windows for high profile customers in very large homes in rich neighborhoods.

I went from being vulnerable, insecure and letting my customers take advantage of me.

To growing a backbone, being confident and knowing the true value of my

my hard work and my service.

And... Made some pretty decent money as well...

So can you!!

You can do it too. Let me repeat this, and I'm making a huge promise right up front.

You can totally do this too....and even more so.

Keep reading.

Because if you want to start a window cleaning business I promise you this book will change your life forever.

Because if you keep reading, this is what you'll learn.

1.) Current state of Window Cleaning Business / How some window cleaners make a ton of money and others don't
2.) (Good News)How the window cleaning business has changed and how exciting it is
3.) (Bad News) is that Most Window Cleaners don't succeed
4.) Talk about (Who wins and who loses) in this new world "Integrity, Authenticity"
5.) Biggest Obstacles that people face..
6.) How to make a ton of money in the Window Cleaning Business
7.) Tools Techniques and tips
8.) Pricing and selling tips
9.) How to actually set up and register your business
10.)How to market your business online and offline

And much more more.
Give me the permission to be your coach, strap yourself in, and welcome to
The Window Cleaning Blueprint.

Also, if you go to www.WindowCleaningBlueprint.com.
There's an entire video training course online that goes along with this book.
Including property walks, on the job training and real time pricing videos.

Chapter 1

The Current State of the Window Cleaning Business

The window cleaning industry is huge. In fact, $40 Billion dollars a year in the U.S alone is spent on cleaning services.

Tons of homeowners who are too busy working long days and taking care of their families have the time to clean their windows. Tons of businesses don't have to staffing or skills to clean their own windows and tons of builders who install windows don't have the connections to get freshly installed windows cleaned.

Churches need window cleaning, city building, car dealerships, real estate properties, fast food places, large homes, small home, nursing centers etc.

The opportunity is literally everywhere because windows are everywhere. This is a huge and exciting realization!

How Things Have Changed

Things aren't like they used to be. In window cleaning or any other business.
Yes you'll still need a squeegee, a scrubber, some towels and eventually an entire van full of window gear.

But what I'm referring to is the playing field of the internet and online marketing.
Back in the day, everything was print advertising, Yellowbook, word of mouth and passing out flyers and business cards.

Although nothing beats walking directly into a plaza storefront and selling your services face to face. There's a new wave of internet savvy entrepreneurs that we need to compete with.

The Bad News

Even though the window cleaning business is very lucrative and there's a ton of work out there.
There's also some bad news.
Bad news is, If you're starting from nothing. You maybe have little to no money, no business experience and are not comfortable handling tons and tons of rejection.

This combined with the new internet marketing paradigm, can wind you down a deep rabbit hole that will make starting and succeeding in the window cleaning business seem impossible.

I get messages everyday from guys who are just getting started. They say "Keith? How in the hell did you get 42 accounts in 48 hours?". "I'm trying to sell, but these storefront

owners won't sign up for window cleaning". or " They said that they already have a window cleaner".
"How do I afford to pay taxes and get insurance when I can't even get the work?"

To tell the truth. The window cleaning business can seem like a discouraging nightmare in the beginning if you don't understand the playing field.

A New Approach

Clearly people are failing and an entirely new approach is needed in order to conquer and make money in this industry. An entirely new way of learning is now necessary to make success even possible in today's marketplace.

There are plenty of other window cleaning guides, how to books, videos and resources online and in paperback.
But as far as I'm aware. No one has actually ever said. "Say this and do that". What I mean is a systematic sequenced approach. Like, literally breaking down the process of what to actually say to a potential new customer in order to land the job, right there on the spot.

Exactly how to clean windows when inside the customer's home. How to conduct yourself in order to differentiate yourself from other companies and most of all. How to market your company online and offline in order to communicate trust, expertise and authority.

This internet marketing thing is huge my friend and it's constantly changing.
We must approach this in an entirely new way. With a mindset that's focused on marketing and innovation, just as much as cleaning the actual windows.

Who Wins and Who Loses in this New World

In this new world. There are going to be people who win and people who lose.
The people who win will know why they're winning. But the people who lose will have no idea why they're losing and will be frustrated.

The people who succeed are going to be the small business owners who can adapt quickly to the ever changing internet marketing paradigm. Those who win will have true authenticity and integrity like never before. In other words, today we are drowning in information overload. There are lies, fluff and corporate advertising everywhere from every different angle.

The amount of information online doubles every 48hrs. and now people have developed a sixth sense. In other words, they can smell bull from a mile away. So communicating very high levels of integrity and professionalism will cut you through the mix fast. People can smell a pro a mile away too. Especially on the internet!

Those who win will learn and develop the art of excellent customer service.

Those who win will implement new technologies faster than other window cleaners.

Who Loses?

All these truths shall be self-evident right? Wrong. Truth is. Most new small business owners aren't aware of how their acting and communicating with their clients because their too caught up in the "Needing Money" paradigm.

So those who don't pay attention to or resist marketing online and those who don't act like professionals will lose.

This is the exact opposite. Those who will lose are the ones who don't have a vicious appetite for success. who refuse to study and learn today's new online environment.

Those who don't learn the basics of SEO, organic online marketing, social media marketing, don't wear professional work attire, act professional, don't track the stats going on in their businesses or treat their window cleaning businesses like professional businesses.

Get what I'm saying? If instead of feeling like you're new window cleaning business is just a hobby for extra cash, you take it very seriously and treat is like a professional business. You'll get dramatically different results. When you quantify these attributes inside an online environment, it magnifies the effects.
So, the people who aggressively learn online advertising, promote their businesses on the internet and act like true

professionals, instead of "the local neighborhood guy who just cleans the windows", will win.

That's you. you will Win!

How I figured it all out

I must have spent 50 hours reading, researching and watching videos on how to start a window cleaning business. But I was frustrated because I literally could only find one guy who actually had guts enough to tell the truth.

Or at the type of truth that I like to hear, and that's none other than Don Marsh.

I found this guy on YouTube.

He was giving clear cut precise advice about how to have a backbone and not let your customers walk all over you as a solo window cleaner.

One day it dawned on me. I was on the phone with my buddy Brandon from AFC Window Cleaning. I was upset and complaining about how I wasn't making any money cleaning windows and didn't know why people would even want to pay anymore than I was currently getting for window cleaning.

He said one thing that changed my life. he said...Keith, "Window Cleaning is a Luxury Service" and your job is to look for people with disposable income. "You're too busy trying to convince people to let you clean their windows, instead of looking for people who have disposable income and already want their windows cleaned".

Aha! Man, that one statement changed the game for me and if you read that last paragraph over and over, I think you'll get it too.
Keep reading.

Chapter 2

My Story of Struggle

I won't go too deep into this. But just to let you know that I'm real and that my intention is to help you start a window cleaning business.
I want you to understand that I know what it's like to truly struggle.

In the beginning days.
In my family, we grew up very poor. As a boy I remember living in homeless shelters, sleeping in a car with my mother, being on welfare, running away at a young age and sleeping on couches.
I've worked tons of dead end jobs for low pay.

I've been fired from more jobs than I can remember. I've been broke, depressed and even hated myself at times. Mostly because I was ashamed that even after years of hard work and hard trying. I still found myself broke and frustrated.
And starting a Window Cleaning business only amplified those insecurities.

Man I tell you I was going out there and getting slaughtered. I didn't know what to charge, I didn't have the nice professional tools, I didn't have receipts to give customers. I was a mess and I needed money. I needed money so bad that I forced myself to figure it out.

I could tell you about all the books I read that helped me out.
"In this book I will give you an entire list of resources".

I Could talk about about the frustrations, rejections, discouragement and eventual breakthroughs.

But there's no doubt that starting and succeeding the window cleaning business took me some serious self-reflection in order to really buckle down and commit to actually making the whole thing work.

Finding a Solution

It all really came down to one thing.
MASSIVE ACTION!
Massive action without hesitation.

Yes, I went out there and made a fool of myself.
I tried every thing, said everything and even cleaned people's windows after they told me no,
I was that over needy guy begging to clean your windows.
I was the over confident fake guy who needed to wanted to clean your windows.
I was the shy insecure repulsive guy who wanted to clean your windows.
I was the weird guy who just plain shared too much information to try to manipulate you into letting me clean your windows.
I was the pushy salesy annoying guy who wanted to clean your windows
and I was the super professional "shirt-tucked-in-with-clipboard" guy who wanted to clean your windows.

The thing I learned that somehow magically made me "Figure it all out" was nothing other than trial and error.
Trial and error combined with Massive freaking action dude.
This is just one of those types of businesses were sitting around thinking about it or being too afraid to take action will not get you anywhere.
Thinking too much or too deep into selling window cleaning jobs will put you into analysis paralysis.

In order to make an omelette, you have to crack a couple eggs right? Well That's how I figured it all out. I got a stack of cheap business cards...and went up and down the main streets of my city and started banging on doors relentlessly screaming "Hey!, Let me clean you windows".

Then everything else literally fell into place on it's own accord.

My Success Story

I went from being scared, vulnerable and coming home exhausted with lint in my pocket,
to cleaning homes in high end neighborhoods making $1,500 profit in a day and an average of $350-$500 minimum profit every day we clean windows.

That's,with just one crew. So when you expand the business, there's obviously more room for more high profit with low overhead.

I went from having an eviction notice on my front door and arguing with my wife over money issues.
To taking us out to eat at a nice restaurant and giving her a dozen roses on Valentine's day… with a box of chocolates and a card too.

I went from banging on doors and coming up with scripts and schemas as how to convince people to let me clean their windows, to people calling me on a consistent basis from happy referrals.

Now, with the popularity of my Youtube videos, I get dozens of emails and messages on social media from friends all over the world telling me how my videos have helped them start their window cleaning businesses. I even do personal coaching and consultation over the phone to help them get the ball rolling.

Chapter 3

The Big Picture of Overview of How a Window Cleaning Business Works

Aside from buying a squeegee and practicing cleaning windows in your own front room for 5 hours straight.

Aside from watching window cleaning YouTube videos and learning all the different techniques of how to actually clean windows.

Aside from mixing vinegar and Dawn dish soap with water to create your own cheap window cleaning solution.

To be effective and run a successful window cleaning business.
There's 5 main things you need to pay attention to when starting any small business..
They are.

  1.) You
  2.) Your market
  3.) Your marketing
  4.) Your people
  5.) Your systems

That's it.

*In order to keep it simple. My attempt here is to describe a framework that will help you
clearly understand the different modalities of the components
of a small business.*

1.) You

Develop the skills and habits necessary to maintain, peace of mind, healthy emotions, awareness, self-discipline, positive attitude, perseverance, hope. etc.

Being in control of yourself, taking care of your mind and body, having a warrior mentality and being proactive are the only things that will bring you through the extremely frustrating and challenging times.

Owning small business will bring the best and worst out of you, so taking care of "you" and constantly being willing to transcend the growing pains are to me the first and most important factor. Otherwise, frankly nothing else works.

2.) Your Market

Determining your market first of all will be at the center of a profitable business.

First of all. Window cleaning is a luxury service.
Let me repeat that.
Window cleaning is a luxury service.
In case you didn't hear me, i'll repeat this one more time.
Window Cleaning is a luxury service.

I distinctly remember being frustrated while growing my business because certain customers wanted to pay so little for window cleaning.

So. If you're starting your business in a low income area, then you'll have to determine who in that area will want their windows cleaned?
It may be strictly small business owners. Or maybe you'll have to get in at really low prices and do a sub-standard quality job, but have 3 times the amount of volume.

If it's high traffic city district then Great. there's plenty of work if you can learn how to sell yourself,
Upper-middle class in my opinion is the sweet spot. these people are educated, make good money and are super busy.

Upper class affluent rich neighborhoods are also great cash cows, but take slightly more advanced marketing and people skills to get into.

3.) **Your Marketing**

One of the most important things in business period is marketing. Without marketing, you barely even have a business. Your marketing should actually be treated as a small business within itself.
Marketing is a huge subject, but I'll tell you this.

All marketing should should be self- taught. Do not rely on other strictly to come up with your marketing and business communication.

Marketing is how you communicate with your potential customers. From graphic design, advertisements, brochures, flyers door hangers, online media, video, print and even how you treat your customers and perform your work is all marketing.

Learning marketing which i'll teach the basics in this book, will be the lifeblood of your business.

4.) Your people

If you're a solopreneur great! As long as you're motivated and can learn all the other principles of running a small business that's actually effective. You should be able to make good money.

If you want to grow your business and get to the point where your only selling jobs and collecting money, then learning how to deal with and manage people will be in my opinion the greatest obstacle to overcome. Learning how to hire, manage, train, support and develop a winning team with your people will be the most challenging and financially rewarding part of your business.

It can also be the biggest nightmare.

5.) Your systems

Your systems are your processes, when the clock is ticking. the most important matter at hand is how the work is actually being done. How effective the work is being done and how smart is the work being done.

having an effective process and protocol when inside of a customers house will turn a 4 hour job into a 2 hour job ending in better quality end result, no tools left behind on jobsites, all windows closed and locked, 5 star reviews and payment collected from customers and a much smoother predictable process.
Having an effective and documented process will eliminate a lot of the surprises from your business. It will also make things go smoother and eliminate a lot of stress.

Your Biggest Obstacles

The biggest obstacles people face when starting a window cleaning business is that

A.)Even though they have all the tools and information necessary,
they don't believe they can do it. or they don't believe it will work for them.
B.) They don't have any mentors
C.) They can't get themselves to commit
D.) They don't have a big enough reason why.
E.) They don't have enough time
F.) They Don't know how much to charge customers
G.) They're afraid of failing (again)
H.) They're afraid of selling door to door
I.) They don't have any startup money.

How to overcome these obstacles

First of all I'm going to cut right through all the crap and say. You can have all the tools and information in the world necessary to get your window cleaning business off the ground. But if you just plain can't get yourself to buckle down and do it, then it's never going to work.

Procrastination is a huge challenge when it comes to the constant bombardment of social media networks, internet, youtube, constantly checking your phone and being addicted to your A.D.D.

I can say that because I definitely struggle with A.D.D and I know how hard it is to deal with the roller coaster of focus issues.

But when you face the brutal reality and realize that your back is against the wall and you need to take action now. That's when the action starts taking place.

Then once you develop the habit of taking action consistently, it gets easier from there.

Let's say your time broke. You already work a full time job that you hate and don't even have the energy to get this thing off the ground.

I was there too and I realized that nothing will ever change in my life until I change it.

To my amazement, I was able to replace my job income a lot faster than I thought.

I can't promise you the same results as me.

But I was so desperate that I went out and sold 42 accounts in 48 hours.

In the beginning I went out and was making $40, $70, $80, $110, $150, $170 a day.

Just by going door to door and hustling small business owners with a squeegee and bucket in my hand.

I knew that another $10-$12 dollar an hour. job would end me up not only failing miserably, but living in my wife's mother's basement.

See what I mean? I don't know your reason why, but for me this was an emergency.

Ok, Let's overcome more of these very real obstacles one at a time.

Let's say you have all the information and tools that you need and

all of that information is right here in this book.

"Hopefully you got the companion (Window Cleaning Blueprint) video course and audiobook too"

Then information isn't stopping you. Maybe you don't feel like you any mentors and only a real person. A real coach has to actually show you what to do in order for it to make sense to you.

Hey!, that's why I'm here. If you'll allow me to be your coach. I'll show you step by step how to do this thing. How to start a Window Cleaning Business, How to actually clean the windows. What tools you need to get started, what to charge, how to get referrals, how to market your business and how to even register and get insurance for your business.

I you're just plain afraid of failing, afraid of spending months of your life and lots of potential money just to find out that you'll end up at the end of a another dead-end road. But this time you won't be able to get out? haha, I had all those fears too. Let me ask you, why did you even buy this book then? What was the spark that had you believing even for a moment that you could actually pull this thing off? Fear of failure is totally paralyzing and if you want the truth. I even have some fear about writing this book right now.
"What if it doesn't sell? what if I invested all this time and energy and money into writing this book and no one even buys it? Maybe I should just stick to cleaning windows and mind my own business" lol. All these thoughts are normal. But if I didn't take a chance and write the book, then you wouldn't even be reading this right now. See, it's tied in purpose. When you search your heart realize that success is not guaranteed. You make your own damn success by being willing to go farther and reach higher than anyone else is. Secret is. most people aren't willing to put in the effort to be a professional. To be world class.

If you're willing to fully commit and put in the work to learn the skills necessary. You'll succeed. It's as simple as that.

Afraid of selling door to door

This can be a tough one. If you're an introvert and you're totally afraid to look someone in their eyes and be confident when you're selling your services. Then..,.I have an interesting spin for you.

What if you weren't selling at all? What if you were just showing up, creating value, providing information and giving them a price? What if instead of a salesperson, you were an educator?

What if you made a fun game out of it? There's no doubt going door to door with a squeegee in your hand is a daunting task. But when you take the neediness and despair in your voice and body language and instead practice having a sense of certainty. That's when you'll start locking down these accounts and making money.

I Don't Have Any Startup Money

Guess what? that makes two of us. When I started my window cleaning business I was flat broke with an eviction notice. All I had was $50 and a small business opportunity magazine. That $50 was actually bill money. My back was against the wall. I tried and tried to find a winter job here in Michigan and went all around town filling out applications.

It was such a bad experience that I can't even stand talking about it.

Chapter 4

How to Start a Window Cleaning Business

I promise I'll get to the point and fill your head with money making information.
But first I want to ask you why you're starting a window cleaning business?
Of all things, all opportunities....
A flippin window cleaning business? Really?

"YES Keith! That's what I'm saying" Alright, now that i got your attention.
I'm going to give you two answers. One the short and sweet version, the other, \
the Long and not so sweet version.

Both work and both will lead you to success... NOT!
So... Here's the short version.

1.) Come up with a name for your new business.
2.) Go to Lowes, Home Depot, Menards or a department store and buy
3.) Scrubber, squeegee, extension pole, ladder, Dish soap and a bucket.
4.) Register an LLC on www.Legalzoom.com with your new Window Cleaing Business Name.
5.) Go to your bank and open a small business account.
6.) Find an insurance agent and get general liability insurance for your new business

7.) Find a graphic designer and get your new Logos, Business cards, website and flyers printed and… start passing them out

8.) Hit the streets and start cold calling everyone in your city including friends and family

9.) Post ads on Craiglist, join chamber of commerce, put ads in local newspaper

10.) Go to Home Depot or Lowes and buy a squeegee, scrubber, bucket and dish soap

11.) Start Cleaning windows and collecting money.

12.) Reinvest the money back into your business. Get a water fed pole too.

Tadaa! Now you're a big success.

THE END…I'm serious here. that's why you bought this book didn't you?

Chapter 5

The Story of Struggle

I'm serious here. Were going to go into everything about starting a window cleaning business, I promise. But I believe that everything starts with you. The biggest issues sometimes don't lie within have the right information on a topic, but more so with actually getting yourself to buckle down and do the thing.

If you ever read my last book called "How to Start a Landscaping Business
RIGHT NOW With NO Startup Money".
I go pretty deep into this whole Fear/Motivation paradigm.

Some people gave me shit about it saying I was rehashing old motivational topics.
But I beg to differ. The truth that people will do more to avoid pain than to get pleasure is the truest saying I've ever heard.

When you're about to lose everything or your freedom is under threat, you have two options.
Fight or Flight….Listen.

  I remember back in 2001 after 911 hit. I was 18 years old and had my first apartment.
This Place was a pretty decked out for an 18 year old kid. I had white leather wrap around sofas…"Which I garbage picked", this huge entertainment center with smoked glass doors and this super nice brand new kitchen table set "Both were on furniture store credit cards" and big tropical plants to make me feel successful. haha.

When my friends would come over, they couldn't believe it. How was Keith so successful at such a young age? Well, truth was. I was working 4 jobs and was stressed out of my wits.

I thought the secret to being successful was to work 100 hours a week. I actually believed that I was a piece of shit if I didn't work constantly.

I remember coming home from my 3rd job at 3am, walking into my apartment and collapsing onto the kitchen floor. I slept 2-3 hours a night for months on end.

When 911 hit. Everything hit the fan and the economy froze for like 3 months. I lost my jobs, lost my income… and found myself going up and down filling out applications everywhere including McDonalds. No one was hiring. The bills kept coming in and I kept on trying. Long story short. I remember lying on the floor in my apartment with an eviction notice in my hand.

I had 30 days to vacate and no money, plus I was now living off my credit cards.

I lost my place, lost my belongings and ended up sleeping in my truck for weeks until a friend let me sleep in his basement. I went $6,500 in debt at the drop of a hat. no ship came to save me.

I tried to move into my mother's house but she was hooked on crack and had strange people living with her.

Fast forward a year later I had gotten back on my feet, but a non-stop tidal wave of life challenges ended me up losing everything and sleeping in my car again. This time for 3 and a half months.

Fast forward to the age of 24. I lost everything again in a bad car accident. racked up enough debt to make someone want to commit suicide and ended up sleeping in another friend's basement.

I took 2 long years but finally got everything back, but never had enough money to pay off the pending debts. In 2009 my mother died of a heroin overdose and I went into depression. In 2010 I got sued and lost everything I owned and ended up on the verge of not only homelessness, but being permanently stuck riding bikes and taking buses for the rest of my life.

I had a nervous breakdown. I locked myself in a dark basement and cried so hard that blood was running from my nose. For the first time I had to face the fact that as smart as I was, as hard working as I was....I was a 27 year old grown man loser. I has no drivers license, no job, no car, no money. I was in a mountain of debt with no way to pay it back and now getting sued
"with payment due immediately", for the amount of money that I was making in an entire year.

There's was no way out. I was going down the hole.

But there was one difference this time…
I had fallen in love and proposed to the girl of my dreams.
I knew that I'd never find anyone like her ever again. She was my soul mate.
I knew that if I fucked this up. I would never recover and never get her back.

I knew that only by the grace of God would I make it out of this thing but if I did.
I made an eternal promise.

That if I was granted just one more chance. Just one more chance at life, Promised that I would be a real man. A man who lived in truth, not denial. A man who would be honest with himself and face his brutal reality. A man who accepted the fact that it's time to grow up.

I went to Home Depot and bought a scrubber, squeegee and a bucket and went up and down the strip malls and plazas in my. I knew nothing about window cleaning. All I knew is that we were totally screwed if I didn't figure out a way to come up with some money.

Window Cleaning is a Huge Market

Window Cleaning is a gigantic business and there's constantly windows that need to be cleaned in every direction you look all day long.

Strip malls, Plazas, storefronts, gas stations, nail salons, pizza shops, restaurants, new construction, residential homes and even large commercial buildings and skyscrapers.

Have you ever just taking a moment to notice how many billions of windows and pieces of glass are everywhere all around you?

There's a part of the brain called the reticular activating system. It basically says when you get a red car you start noticing all of the other red cars on the road.
Same with windows.

The market for Window Cleaning is huge and yes there is tons of competition but don't let that stop you for a single second. I've had countless customers compliment me on how they chose me and stuck with me because of the simple reason that I actually showed up.

Window Cleaning as a service that one needs to be done until the end of time. The market is staring you in the face waiting for you to take a bite out of it.

Your Marketing

I could dive very deep into marketing. But I'll save that for another book.
Your marketing and understanding of marketing will be the lifeblood of your business.
I had an entire chapter about marketing in my previous book "how to start a landscaping business right now with no startup money".

If you haven't read it or at least gotten a copy of the audiobook version. Please grab yourself a copy on Amazon or Audible.com.
There a ton of principles in that book that apply across all small businesses.

Is a new reality when it comes to marketing and the Internet is the future and the future is now.
If you've ever heard about search engine optimization and Google algorithms then you are no longer special.

Today only the most authentic customer service driven, online reputation brand building awareness driven businesses will survive.

In order to cut through the white noise and stand out above the rest. You must be diligent about learning the different modalities of marketing and building an online presence.

Such as having a mobile optimized clean friendly easy to navigate website with clear calls to action touch button dialers, customer testimonials and five star reviews. Also being extremely adamant about passing out door hangers, business cards, flyers, refrigerator magnets and brochures to every single customer and their neighbors as well.

For instance, literally every single customer that you deal with you must send them the link to leave you a positive 5 star review on either Google business or your social media networks or both.

You must take pictures and videos and post them on your social media networks of completed jobs and tag them properly with proper descriptions in order to keep building reputation and brand awareness.

Marketing your business and constant innovation must become a habitual process that is not taken for granted. The extra five minutes per job that it takes two get a 5-star review from a customer and put a refrigerator magnet on their table must be built into the time for each job and also calculated as billable hours.

The only way you're going to get to the point of making minimum $500 a day in this business is by doing something I call expanding the top as you dissolve the bottom.

By constantly and consistently marketing your business online and offline your directing traffic through a sales funnel process that is constantly qualifying new prospects and turning them into customers and then turning those customers into clients. But along the way you're going to scrape your knees, get bruised and learn a lot of long hard lessons about what it takes to actually achieve success in not only the window cleaning business but any small business. You're going to encounter cheap frugal sarcastic customers who don't respect you, look at you like the scum of the earth, try to take advantage of you, and blatantly rip you off by trying to get you to do stuff for free.

I'm not trying to be negative here but when you first get started in the window cleaning business there is some confidence issues that comes along with playing this game. When I first got started in the window cleaning business I was broke, needy, and insecure. I attracted fearful, negative, whiny picky clients and customers.

I remember pulling my hair out and going home completely discouraged and wanting to give up and quit every other day because I didn't believe that there was any money to be made in this business.

These negative belief patterns went on for months until I found myself a mentor. Well actually there were several Mentors a couple of them on the internet but one of them in real life.

#1. Brandon from AFC Window Cleaning here in Michigan. We became friends early on and I subcontracted some work for from him cleaning windows inside of the mall and even cleaning the new construction in a large bank.

It's funny because after sweeping and cleaning the windows in that bank the construction guys were sawing wood the very next day and got wood dust all over the windows. I had to go back and reclaim the entire job again for free in order to get paid.

Are used to call Brandon up when I was in emergencies and cry to him about how I wasn't making any money and these customers are so damn cheap.
Then he would school me tell me the most powerful information that I needed in that moment.
I'm totally appreciative of him because the number one thing he ever told me is this.

**"Keith, Window Cleaning is a luxury service. Your job is to market to and find affluent people in rich neighborhoods with disposable income who can afford to spend top dollar on a luxury cleaning service.
Stop wasting your time running around cleaning windows for peanuts because you'll never make any money".**

Window Cleaning is a luxury service

So listen to me clearly because this has everything to do with marketing your new business. When you communicate that you're a professional legitimate business who's done work 4 tons of high end clients in high-profile neighborhoods. When you take this business like a serious career and consider yourself a professional instead of some dude who just cleans windows.

That's when other people will take you seriously and you'll start Landing the $500 + jobs.

Let's go into the different modalities of marketing now.

This chapter will be similar to some stuff on my old book but also new stuff because a lot has changed since then.

In the meantime

Here's some awesome, famous and very informational
Window Cleaners
I want you to check out .

Lee Burbidge - Window Cleaning Magazine
www.WindowCleaningMagazine.co.uk
Look him up on YouTube also

And

Joshua Latimer
Founder of Automate Grow Sell and
The Quick Talk Podcast
http://quicktalkpodcast.com/

And

If you want to watch and learn from a window cleaner who is a *technical genius.*
Lookup **"Luke the Window Cleaner"** on Youtube!

Chapter 6

YOUR MARKETING

If you don't know jack about marketing, well now is the time to learn.
Marketing is what makes the phone ring.
Marketing is How you communicate to the world that you're in business.
Marketing (Just like Money) is the OXYGEN of your business.

You have to start marketing your business for visibility purposes, because
the more visible you are... the more the phone rings.. the more quotes you
book... the more jobs you sell... the more jobs you complete... the more
money you make.

Marketing is you standing on your soapbox and
repeatedly yell... *"HEY EVERYONE... I'M IN BUSINESS".*

NAMING YOUR BUSINESS

To me... this is obvious...Name your business something cool, or you last
name or something.

(Not giving legal advice here)
Example: Johnny's Window Cleaning . tadaa..
Don't name it something stupid.. Lol

METHODS OF MARKETING

Below is a list of all the (NO cost to HIGH cost) ways you can use to market
your business. We also calls these "Lead Sources"

YOUR MARKETING TOOLBOX
TANGIBLE DIY (Low-Cost)
1. Business Cards
2. Door Hangers
3. Flyers
4. Postcards
5. Brochures
6. Magnets
7. Stickers
8. Pens
9. Coffee Mugs
10. Bandit Signs

INTERNET (No-Cost)
1. Craigslist Ads
2. YP.com
3. Angies List
4. Yelp
5. Google Places for Business
6. Bing
7. Yahoo
8. YellowBot

9. Yahoo
10. MapQuest
11. Your Website

SOCIAL MEDIA (No-Cost)
1. Facebook Business Page
2. Twitter
3. Linkedin
4. Pinterest
5. Instagram
6. YouTube
7. Myspace.
8. Vine
9. Google+
PRINTED MEDIA (Medium-Cost)
1. Newspaper
2. Magazines
3. Trade Magazines
4. Direct Mailings
5. Coupons
6. Save-On Magazines
7. Community Mailers
8. Coffee Shop Digests
BROADCAST MEDIA (High-Cost)
1. Radio
2. Television
3. Cable TV

DON'T SPEND MONEY ON MARKETING

At first....
Developing an obsession with finding
NO-Cost or LOW-Cost ways to
market your Window Cleaning business will really paid off for
you in a big way.

How do I know this? Because I was flat broke.
I didn't have a dollar to
spare so I was forced to figure this stuff out on my own.

I found an amazing book that I recommend called "Guerilla
Marketing" by Jay Conrad Levinson.
It's all about Low Cost or No
cost ways to market your business.

This book had me running around like a mad man putting wire
bandit signs
in the Michigan turnarounds of busy intersections, passing out
business
cards, approaching total strangers, and building social media
profiles until
my eyes bled.
What I'm saying is you can totally market your business for
close to free in the beginning.
Speaking of free...Want to get the phone ringing right now?

Craigslist is a Pot of Gold

I don't disagree that craigslist can be like fishing in the toilet.
Also be aware that everyday that passes, Craigslist will
become more more saturated and less and less powerful.

But that doesn't negate the fact that it still works and if you don't have a marketing budget this is stop number 1.

I've built my entire business off of Craigslist ads.
Even some of my best friends I've met off Craigslist.
Yes Man! If you want to get your business rolling fast. Create like 4 email
addresses and then create 4 Craigslist accounts.
Then Start posting your ass off.

You probably have seen my YouTube channel and I have a famous video called
("12 Craigslist Ads a Day")
Some people got upset with me over that video because I basically promoted spamming on the Internet. But my main intention was to explain and teach how to get out of the hole if you're starving to death and need money fast.

So take into consideration some of the things that I teach are coming from a very specific state of consciousness and not intended for general everyday use A well oiled business.

How to Post ads on Craigslist

Start out by taking the digital image of your business card and using as the
main pic in your posting. If you don't have business cards yet you can hire a graphic designer and get them printed on

vistaprint.com
uprinting.com
fiverr.com
elance.com
odesk.com
Up work.com
Etc

Then either take pictures of your real work or steal them from Google images.
Pictures of windows being cleaned,
Sunny skies etc.

Anything to make your business look legit.
So a Sample Craigslist Ads
looks Like this.

DISCLAIMER: This is basic beginners marketing copy and serves a basic
purpose. We're not going to get into marketing psychology and
high-persuasion selling techniques.
So... thru the eyes of Top Marketing Experts like Dan Kennedy.

This Ad is Lame and non-enticing.
Learning how to post million dollar ads…
Comes in time.
If you want to learn more about marketing here are some phenomenal references that have changed my life.

Dan Kennedy - No BS Marketing
Eben Pagan - Modern Marketing Mastery
Jay Conrad Levinson - Guerilla Marketing Tactics
Joe Polish - Piranha Marketing Experts

Below is an example Craigslist Ad to get the ball rolling.

1.) create a free account on Craigslist.
2.) post ad in either small business services or gig section.

Subject Line:
Johnny's Window Cleaning
All Exterior Windows Cleaned $99
for (YOUR CITY)

or
Window Cleaning (Best Deals in Town)

Content:

Johnny's Window Cleaning
"We Out Shine the Best"
1(888)555-1212
Proudly Serving the (YOUR CITY) area
- Window Cleaning
- Gutter Cleaning
- Chandelier Cleaning
- Light Fixture Cleaning

Ask about our $99 Home Cleaning this month
Call 1(888)555-1212
Johnny - Owner
Licensed and Insured Highly Referred.

MAYBE:
A short company bio.. like…

"Established in 2011,
Johnny's Window Cleaning company has been cleaning
windows for residents of your Township and is part the City
Chamber of Commerce and even participates in the local
neighborhood festival every year.

Has cleaned properties in (YOUR CITY). Johnny's Window
Cleaning guarantees results to
its clients and is licensed insured-highly referred."

Now,
Unless this looks professional, don't try it...
But if you can pull it off, the older people love this stuff and it
will give them
an instant sense of trust.

There you go.

Now posting new and slightly different Ed everyday for the
next day until you have 3 ads.
 now take an entirely different email address and create
another Craigslist account.
 repeat this process with multiple email addresses in multiple
Craigslist accounts until you have a system in place where

you can post around three times a day from three different accounts.

WARNING: you should only be posting this much on Craigslist if you're totally desperate and need work right now.

consistently posting this much will not only make your competitors and possibly potential clients hate you but will also get your ads ghosted on Craigslist. Ghosted means "turned invisible".

I post 3 ads on Craigslist every morning as soon as I wake up.

Then I posted three more ads while eating lunch.

if I'm feeling really aggressive a post 3 more eggs in the evening around 6pm. but rest assured I am always posting on Craigslist every single day no matter what.

Enough of Craigslist I'm sick of talking about Craigslist.

Paid Marketing

 the truth is the most effective form of marketing is paid marketing and advertising. like I said marketing and advertising are an entire business within themselves and you can spend your life time studying them. I personally AM obsessed with marketing. I've spent thousands of hours reading books, watching seminars, and paying for marketing programs that has completely changed my life and perceptions of the world as we know it.
 if I could touch your forehead and show you how deep and in-depth marketing and advertising actually goes and how much our entire world is affected over and over again because of it…

So anyways you can place an ad in the local newspaper people will probably call you if it's the time of season that calls for what you're advertising. Advertising just puts a big magnifying glass on what's going on in your market anyways. if it's springtime and everybody wants their windows cleaned, then putting out advertisements will make your phone blow up off the hook.

 if it's the middle of the winter and nobody wants their windows cleaned, then spending a million dollars on advertising will be a complete waste of your money.
 okay although print media still works such as door hangers flyers business cards brochures and stuff like that.
Nothing really compares to the power of advertising online because for one, it lasts longer. Investing in advertising online holds more weight and value longer because it's in digital cloud-based format and has a lot longer life cycle than print.

I could go really deep into this.

I suggest investing in everything you possibly can that's free or next to free.
Only when you've created enough revenue to afford an advertising budget should you start signing contracts with marketing companies.

Here's some companies that work.
In no specific order.

1,) Yodle
2.) Yelp
3.) YP
4.) Google Business
5.) Google Ads
6.) Home Advisor
7.) Angies List
8.) Townsquare
9.) Signpost
10.) Thumbtack

These are just to mention a few, but truth is. All of these companies want money.
Some of these companies want you to sign a minimum of a 6 month contract of a $200 minimum.
Don't get me wrong. All of these companies work. They're like hiring virtual assistants or ad agencies to do and manage your marketing for you. If you were to hire someone in house to do your marketing for you. You'd easily be paying $1,000 month for someone who probably doesn't even know what the hell their doing.

With these big marketing companies, You get to hire professional marketing team virtually who will build you a website, get your page ranked on google, manage customer relationships, make your phone ring, generate referrals. on and on,

So in conclusion. The longer you sit on the pot being afraid to sign contracts with these marketing companies is the better and faster chance that your competition is going to figure out that
"This is the new way".   In fact, they're already doing it. Take a look online and type
"Window Cleaning" into Google.
All the companies that pop up in the first 3 positions are on their marketing SEO A-Game and also spending serious dollars on all of these rank advancement and engagement services.

Search Engine Optimization

If you don't know what this is then you better hire someone fast.
Google has Penguin and Panda algorithms that are constantly being updated.

Today, paying for facebook likes, twitter followers and what's considered "Black hat" SEO Techniques, will get your page demoted and crippled inside of Google's Search engines, You must do pretty much 90% all organic marketing now in order to get ranked and stay there.

That means creating a blog on www.Wordpresss.org alongside your website for your business.
Making sure all of your sites are routinely being updated with fresh pictures, videos and keyword rich content that's backed by organic local customer engagement.

For instance. You want to do all this on a drip-feed system. Don't just upload 20 videos and a bunch of 5 star Google reviews all in one day to your website, blog, social media networks and Google Review site. Doing this will make you look like you're trying to cheat the system.

Simulate everything as if it were happening in real-time.
The reason I'm telling you this is because if you're not doing this, you need to start right now.
Like immediately.
If you want to have a successful Window Cleaning Business. Then building brand awareness and growing a positive reputation online is urgent.

Chapter 7

Only The Strong Survive

This Will Be Physically Hard

There's no lie if you're used to doing manual labor then you know what it's like to work your ass off from Sun up till sundown and come home in pain.

From the outside cleaning windows seems like you would be easy but actually I would argue that it's just as physically hard or harder as any other physical labor job.

Of course you have to work your ass off to be successful in anything but what I'm talking about here is efficiency. There's a certain system in way that you must move your body and take into account every single physical action and step you take in order to get a job done quickly and by conserving as much physical energy as possible.

Hauling around heavy ladders tote bins, Window Cleaning gear, squeegees, walking all over properties and climbing up and down ladders non stop for 10 hours a day 5 to 6 days a week can burn you out to the point where you can't get out of bed.
I learned this the hard way and I don't want you to make the same mistake. For instance I used to clean a bunch of stores inside of strip malls and plazas.
Like an idiot I would walk back and forth to my truck to get a sip of water or grab another window cleaning tool or grab the receipt for the customer and didn't realize how much time I was wasting.

If you want to get into the deeper reason why I kept walking back to my truck it's because my self esteem was low.
I was tired and trying to get away from the pain and suffering of the brutal reality of the financial situation I was facing.

Without going too deep into what I just said.
I think the reason men are late for work or do a bad job.
Or do weird things at work is more about the inner conflict that's going on in their minds and their emotions and less about their ability to do the actual job.

So starting a window cleaning business and growing it takes a lot of certainty. You must have a vision and must remain excited because the amount of rejection coming your way is enough to make anyone want to crawl into a corner and quit.

The amount of rejections you're going to get are going to either be the fuel that drives you to keep refining your selling process or be like wounds that you carry around with you.

So let's combine your actual process of cleaning the windows with your emotional state and move forward.

How to Sell Jobs On the Spot

In my years of being in business I've learned that sequence is everything. I know I'm going on and on here but I want you to understand if you do things in the wrong order you will bang your head against the wall.

1.)Make sure you have business cards a pen your cell phone and a receipt book with you.
You can get business cards at www.vistaprint.com or www.uprinting.com.

You can acquire a receipt book at Office Depot, Office Max or any office supply store or even Walmart.
If you really want to get fancy.
Get a subscription to QuickBooks Mobile on your smartphone and actually send them professional email invoices while simultaneously collecting their email address for future marketing purposes.

For the most part strip-mall storefront and Plaza owners such as franchise sub shops you might not be dealing with the manager and it will be an employee that hand you cash out of the register.

Once again in this book I'm not going to get too deep into finance and accounting.

The Script

1.) Walk into a local store front
2.) Ask for the manager or owner
3.) If the manager or owner is not present give your presentation anyways.
4.) When the owner walks out smile and say
5.) "Hi, my name is Joe, I only local window cleaning business and we're expanding in this area. Your windows look dirty. Do you currently have anybody who cleans your windows.   It doesn't matter what they say "yes no maybe so" very very busy and 90% of the time going to try to push you away and get you out of the store.
6.) In no means does this mean that they don't want their windows cleaned. It just means that they're busy and are annoyed or distracted by your presence Note: if you are really excited and have positive expectancy you can overcome this and actually make them excited to talk to you.
7.) They say. " yes we already have someone who cleans the windows"
8.) **NO MATTER WHAT THEY SAY. YOU SAY**
9.) Great, are they reliable and are you happy with their services?
10.)   No matter what they say you say "great I can match their price or even do it for cheaper and I can clean them right here right now on the spot...whaddya say"?

11.) If they say yes then you say great. Grab your tools and clean all the windows right then and there. Write them a receipt. Then say "great I'll see you in two weeks"

12.) Be very assumptive, no contracts or anything, if they say no. Say "no worries I'll be in this area in two weeks. I'll stop in and say hello anyways and if the windows are dirty give me the thumbs up and I'll clean them again". Hand them a business card and be on your way to the next storefront.

13.) If they still say no about having their windows cleaned in the first place, hand them a business card and say, " great, good reliable window cleaners are hard to come by. If your window cleaner ever disappears, give me a call"

14.) Once you build a local reputation and secure a lot of accounts, then you can start earning trust and getting into your customers residential homes.

That's it!

If you go door to door to door to door to door to door like a maniac and say that simple script over and over with confidence, positive expectancy and enthusiasm.
You should be able to get plenty of work.

Also, you would not believe how many customers will call you back later on that day, the next day, or even weeks later wanting you to come clean their windows.

I just want you to take a moment to accept and realize the power of a handshake and a business card. A simple handshake a hello and a business card goes so far and like a rock in a pond makes ripples that you would not believe.

I've gotten tons of jobs from referrals of people that I don't even remember even meeting because of my insatiable habit of shaking hands and passing out business cards.

Real Talk

I encourage you to become a walking talking salesman. From this moment forward you will become a walking talking TV commercial that lives and breathes the selling of your service to every human being imaginable.

I know this sounds extreme but in my case and point, I came from extreme financial problems and facing an eviction notice.

When I met my wife.

It was my responsibility to make damn sure we didn't fail.

I got rid of everything in my life that didn't equal making money. Have you ever heard the saying "if it don't make dollars it don't make sense?" that was my new saying and it changed my life. I sold all of my beloved studio equipment and all the stupid bullshit that was holding me back from being successful.

It's better to I've loved and lost than to have never loved at all. Its also better to have a hobby that you loved and had to give up for the sake of something better.

- Sometimes giving up the things you love in life or letting go of the things that keep you comfortable are necessary in order to grow into something new.
- Like a snake sheds its skin or a rose blooms. It can be very painful, but a rose must bloom or it will die.

If you see my youtube videos I take a lot of pride in sharing my story of the struggle.

When you share the struggle with somebody….
then sharing success with them is that much sweeter.

My hope is that you build a successful window cleaning business and experience the success that you dream of.

Chapter 8

The Pricing Gauntlet

The pricing gauntlet is where you get caught up in frustration and discouragement because you can't figure out how to make any money cleaning windows.
You say. "How in the hell is that guy getting jobs for those high prices? when I can't even find one single customer to even pay a medium price"?

I'm telling you man this is some Karate Kid, mr. Miyagi, Law of Attraction, believe in yourself type of stuff here. If you don't believe it. I promise you it will never come true for you.
I know this stuff because I've been through the pricing gauntlet myself. It's a catch 22 trap that will make you pull your hair out and want to quit this business like a bad habit.

So…

Before you read this chapter I want you to clearly understand that the prices people pay for window cleaning, vary drastically from town to town, from city to city, from Plaza to Plaza, from house to house, from human mind to human mind.

Please listen to me clearly because I don't want to hear you whining and suffering when you're trying your hardest and to no avail, nobody wants to pay you the numbers I'm about to talk about in the upcoming sections of this book.

Repeat after me, "Window Cleaning is a luxury service".

If you waste your time trying to convince people who don't want their windows cleaned to clean their windows, then you're probably not going to make a lot of money.

In the beginning, take every single job you can get.
in the beginning, I want you cleaning old ladies houses for $54 bucks.
Old ladies who have 12 cats that are taking turns sitting on your head while you're cleaning those windows.

But once you start growing, learn how to expand the top while simultaneously dissolving the bottom.

Learn how to keep raising your prices again and again and again and again and again. the more confident and confident you become with your service, is the more your prices need to go up.

The whole point of this business is to eventually get into high end homes and eventually you'll be cleaning entire commercial buildings, churches, and maybe even skyscrapers one day.

But you gotta crawl before you can walk and you gotta walk before you can run.
I promise these results are true because I was flat broke myself, and couldn't believe it when I started making $500 a day cleaning windows.

I want you to take a deep breath, count to 2, exhale. Then imagine what it would be like to make $500 in a single day cleaning windows.

Now here's the truth, after all the frustrating hell you go through of learning this business and actually figuring out how to get inside of these high end homes and actually get people to pay you hundreds of dollars to clean their windows.

You actually get pissed off when you make less than $500 if you spent the entire day cleaning windows.

It's a catch 22 and I don't want you to get caught up in the pricing gauntlet.

How to Price Window Cleaning Jobs

You can get advice from 50 different angles on how to price out window cleaning jobs.

A good rule of thumb is to price your jobs and run your business "as if" your already running a fully legitimate licensed and insured window cleaning company with payroll taxes, workman's compensation, Roth IRA and even extra money for maintaining your vehicles and reinvesting for growth.

"So Keith, you mean to tell me that even though I'm just getting started I have to charge over $100 an hour to clean windows?" Yes that's what I'm telling you.

The hard truth is that if you're totally inexperienced And you don't even portray yourself as a company that stands at that level of professionalism. Then charging $100 an hour to clean somebody's windows right off the bat is insanity.

First of all you got to "get in where you fit in". That's actually one of my favorite sayings and I don't know why, it just makes so much sense.

If you're just starting out like I was, the best option for the quickest money is to get into storefronts, strip malls, and plazas.

In the beginning you have to "whore yourself out", So my buddy Dave calls it.

But it's true, you have to do everything possible in the beginning to simply generate activity in the business. Its called "throwing mud at the wall to see what sticks"

Here Goes Pricing

For storefront strip malls and plazas I'd say 2 to $3 per window inside and out. Yes that's only 1 to $2 per pane. You can argue all you want, but I've personally been there and done that and I'll tell you.

These small businesses and mom and pop shops will laugh at you if you tell them your going to charge them $45 per window to clean their glass, when Joe Blow down the street does it for a buck a window. You will never ever get rich off cleaning storefronts plazas and strip malls Unless your securing the big corporate contracts and dominating at top dollar nationwide.

Yes it's totally possible, but if you're just getting started and you don't know what the hell you're doing, I suggest getting inside strip malls and plazas, working your ass off and making some quick money. "Getting Paid to learn".

So for instance let's say a cell phone store has 12 windows, well you would think something like that goes for 36 bucks. But actually I guarantee you the last window cleaning guy was doing it for 12 to 15 bucks cash. so that means you can come in as confident as you want you can say everything in the book, but there's no way in hell that guy is going to pay you more than $15, $20 bucks to clean the windows.

In the beginning I was cleaning entire restaurants for $32 bucks that would normally go for around $200. I'm not lying dude. I was insanely desperate and would have done anything for a dollar, & I did. I came in at prices so low that you would have thought I was a crackhead. I didn't care I wanted to grow my business and I wanted to make money right now. So what you can offer your customers is what we like to call a "no brainer". Money is the most important part, but I say just get your foot in the door at whatever price possible to start generating cash flow.

So to conclude this section. Cell phone stores 12 to 15 bucks, small restaurants 30 to 40 bucks, hair salons 12 the 15 sometimes 30 bucks, bars and nightclubs 60 bucks. My prices today are literally triple this, and that's why I don't do strip malls, plazas, or storefronts anymore. Because they simply won't hire me. They laugh when I give them a quote. They think I'm joking or something. I want you to eventually get to the same point.

Dissolve the bottom as you expand to the top

Personal Mastery Coach, "Coach Rob" from Ego Edge Taught me this amazing distinction.
You can apply it to any area of the universe. As your business gets healthier and grows, you are expanding the top.
Naturally you'll want to simultaneously dissolve the bottom.

Every single year, as your business gets more legit and you want to invest more in your business appeal. The stakes will get higher as well and you'll need to keep raising prices in order to stay afloat.

Use the "split test" to raise prices

Once again. This is so important, I have to mention it twice. When in doubt, utilize the A/B split test. Split your leads down the middle.
It doesn't Necessarily have to be 50/50. But at some juncture, decide which percentage of your new leads and customers you will raise the price on.

So. half of them gets charged more. The other half stays the same.
If you're having trouble choosing which 50% of your new quotes to raise the price on.
Raise your price on the percentage of customers that live in the nicer homes in the higher-end neighborhoods.

One storefront... walk in... tell them $15. The other storefront you walk into
"same size, different city" tell them $25.

Split tests are used commonly in many places, especially marketing. Some marketers won't even put their stamp of approval on their literature until it has been proven to convert at it's highest percentage through multiple split tests.

A marketing example; would be putting out two advertisements in two different neighborhoods.
One ad that has the original standard price and the other ad that has a higher price.
One ad simply says one thing, while the other ad says another.

This way you are not stuck being one-track minded. *Feeling like you have no other*
options is the way of the poor. Successful people always try to ask themselves. "How can I have both"?

Use split tests whenever possible and don't forget it. Split tests are the best ways to raise prices with the lowest amount of risk.

I like split tests because they didn't occur to me when I started my window cleaning business. I was stuck banging my head against the wall charging everybody the same price. I had to learn about split testing and try it for myself to learn about its magic.

It's just so funny how the simplest things that can make us more profit, go right over our heads.

Chapter 9

You Will See it When You Believe It.

"First You Must Actually Believe That You Can Make a Fortune Cleaning Windows"

When you get into high-end homes and rich neighborhoods, not only are people willing, but they want to pay top dollar for the highest quality service.
in my own window cleaning business, probably one out of every 5 jobs is $400 or higher. I'm not lying when I tell you that I've cleaned windows for 400, 500, 600, 700, 800, and even $900 to clean a
12,000 square foot mansion.

The mansion was glass outside only plus cleaning 10 light fixtures at $20 each.
We were in and out in about 4 hours with the water fed pole system.

Earlier that morning, Myself and one worker cleaned another mansion *outside glass only for $750*. We were in and out in three and a half hours. Plus we picked up our client's neighbors house for $250.

After gas, labor, insurance, and taxes I made $1,550 profit in one day for cleaning flippin windows man.
And I personally don't live in a rich neighborhood. I have to drive an hour one-way to get to the rich neighborhoods, here

in Michigan. So if you're poor, and you grew up in a poor neighborhood. Don't let being poor stop you from becoming rich. Just because we might of come from families who couldn't afford to pay $400 to get our windows cleaned. Doesn't mean for a second that rich people in rich neighborhoods have the same experience.

The longer you're in business, the more wealthy people will hire you.
Being around wealthy people will change your life because over time you learn that aside from love respect and being spiritual. there's not too much that money can't buy.

Extremely busy people who make a lot of money don't have time to be climbing up and down a ladder cleaning their windows. Window cleaning is a luxury service. so start Thinking like your customers and developing a luxury mindset ASAP.

If you've seen my youtube videos. I talk about my friend Brandon who makes $1,000 a day every single day. He's been able to work almost strictly in rich neighborhoods for high profile business owners, CEOs, and famous entrepreneurs and athletes. I almost didn't believe him when he told me he was making $1,000 a day. One day he invited me to come help him clean windows at this gigantic mansion. I'm telling you this house was enormous. We were in and out in four and a half hours.
He showed me the check for $1,560.
Seeing that proof back then even changed my life to what is possible in this business.

Pricing Homes

If you keep cleaning storefronts and plazas. Eventually you'll get into customers residential homes. Only a certain percentage of your window cleaning customers will actually give you the opportunity to clean their homes.
Partly I believe because... there small business owners, and most small business owners are cheap.
The more you tell the world that you're in the business of cleaning windows.
The longer you consistently keep cleaning windows.
The more you picture yourself having $500 days cleaning windows.
Is the sooner it will all happen. I guarantee it.

According to Home Advisor.
The average window cleaning job in terms of national averages
in 2016 was $206.
That means that the average customer paid $206 to have their windows cleaned.

AVERAGE REPORTED COSTS

$206

MOST HOMEOWNERS
SPENT BETWEEN

$149 - $291

LOW COST

$84

HIGH COST
$400

$206 Would be the price of an average two story house with sliding door walls,
 bay windows and a couple garage windows.

Let's just say that it's normally a 1,500 square foot house.

Now remember this is the average price in general. Some homeowners want
what I refer to as "**THE WORKS PACKAGE**".
This includes their window tracks scrubbed out, sills wiped down, screens cleaned and Everything PERFECT.
Others want glass cleaning only.

The lowest average price paid is $84, and that would be a single story ranch.
 Glass cleaning exterior only.
Besides, most customers with small homes don't like paying over $100 anyways.

The average price is usually between $149 - $291 for upper middle class homes in the United States.
Remember, this is the average price combined whether it's just glass cleaning only, or

"the works" package above.

Here's the cool part! The average high price paid of $400 is not a gimmick. this is actually very common in the window cleaning business, It's also downright inspiring.

Residential Homes - Pricing Structure

Choose a Pricing Plan

Check Out Our Latest Specials!	X-Large Homes	Large Homes	M... H...
Premium Package	From	From	

Everything in the Deluxe **Package PLUS** **All tracks vacuumed out** **and screens deep-cleaned.**	**$849**	**$449**	$
Deluxe Package erything in the Basic Package PLUS Interior glass surfaces cleaned, interior sills wiped clean, basic screen ning, and interior tracks wiped clean.	From **$649**	From **$349**	$
Basic Package ning of all your home's **Exterior** glass ces, guaranteeing a streak-free finish. Exterior sills wiped clean.	From **$349**	From **$249**	$

Single Hung Windows
Total Cost: $8.00

Double Hung Windows
Total Cost: $8.00

Casement
Total Cost: $4.00

Geometric Shapes
Total Cost: $4.00

Awnings
Total Cost: $4.00

Single & Double Sliding Windows
Total Cost: $8.00

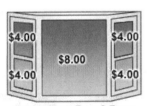

Double Hung Bays & Bows
Total Cost: $24.00

$1.00 per pane

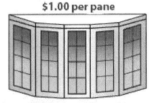

French Windows & French Doors
Total Cost $40.00

Sliding Patio Doors
Total Cost: $15.00

Swinging Patio Doors
Total Cost: $10.00

I really want you to spend some serious time studying the images on the last page.
 If you skimmed over it, stop, go back and study the last two pages.

Learn about the different types of windows, the different shapes of Windows, the different names for these windows and learn how to identify them.

 Prices may vary in different parts of the world. There are also many different brands of Windows. Over 100. But amongst the most common are,
Andersen Corp--carried by Home Depot,
Pella Corp.*--carried by Loews.

There are also 100 different types Of screens and trust me we will go into screens in another section of this book.

 I think the prices above can be confusing if you're just getting started. I think it's easier to just round down or round up to a solid number.

It's easy when you can just walk around a house pointing at windows going "$5, $10, $10, $2, $10, $4,".

I personally go with 3 different rules when quoting a residential window cleaning property.

1.) I walk around the house and count every single window then add up the sum total. Let's say I come up with $200.
2.) Then I go with a standard pricing of about how many square feet the house is. If I don't know how many

square feet the house is I just go with my gut feeling based on price.

3.) My third conclusion comes from calculating labor man hours. Ideally you want to gross $100 an hour or more If you are a one man show. $45 an hour minimum net.

My point is, don't become obsessive over getting the numbers exactly right. just walk around the damn house, count the windows and come up with the price. Make sure the price is approximate and mathematically right, feels right, and also is priced according to the neighborhood and income status of your customer.

But don't get stuck in your head, thinking that your price is already too low, or too high.
 Listen to me closely. What you think or feel has nothing to do with your business.

Also, what you think or feel has nothing to do with how your customer thinks or feels.
 until you're making enough money to afford to run a fully legitimate window cleaning business.

Until you're making enough money to be able to afford to maintain work vehicles, license, insurance, taxes, workmans comp, health insurance, a window cleaning shop, an automatic retirement account and enough money to protect your family and cover them in case something happens to you.

Then you're not charging enough for your services.

Chapter 10

The Mindset Behind Pricing

If you are in a wealthy zip code, charge more. If you are in a middle-class zip code, charge a little less. if you are in a poor zip code. then run like hell, and don't clean windows in poor areas.

I grew up extremely poor. I've lived literally in the ghettos of Detroit. I've lived in the ghettos of the Metro Detroit suburbs. And I've lived in middle class blue collar areas.

Aside from small business owners, storefronts, plazas and small businesses. Very few lower middle class, and middle class people can afford the luxury service of having their windows cleaned.
Also, if they do want their windows cleaned.Then they want it done for a very low price.
The only way you can survive this way is if you.

1.) lower your prices
2.) lower your quality
3.) Come up with a system that allows you and your team to clean the windows really fast.

Similar to lawn care. If you're stuck in a lower class area and want to make a lot of money, you have to bang out a bunch of lawns in a tight area really fast and consistently.

The major difference with window cleaning, is that you can actually see every single spot an imperfection left on the glass.

I hate cutting corners and I've been in anxiety when having to rush around a customer's house.
That's not my style, I'd rather do top notch work for top notch money.

Working your way into upper middle class and rich neighborhoods is really the way to go if you want to make good money in the window cleaning business.

My Perspective
I've done it all man. I've done it all. because even in upper middle class and rich neighborhoods you're still going to deal with all the same frustrations no matter what.

I've seen this over and over. You can have two rich customers who live right next door to each other in the same neighborhood. One of them will want to spend top dollar and even leave you a $50 tip. The other will shoot you down so low that you end up
1.) Hating cleaning his windows,
2.)Never leaves you a tip, and threatens to fire you because he can find someone cheaper.

My favorite saying is "get in where you fit in".

Oh man do I love that saying. to me that means exactly what it says. Having standardized prices is great. It looks great on your website. It looks great on your brochures. And it sounds great coming out of your mouth when speaking to your customers.

There's a certain element of hustle that it takes to be successful in any small business. If you have to give a 1st time customer discount in order to get the job, then do it.

If you want to raise another customers price simply because you want to make more money and for no other reason, Then do it if you can.

 I stand behind these words 100%. these are the words of the wealthy.

Wealthy people make more money simply because they want to.

I'm sure they don't have tons of deep soulful answers as to why.

But if you could charge somebody $5,000 to clean their windows and they actually don't mind paying. By all means, do it.

Small business owners sometimes get stuck in being broke and scrambling for peanuts simply because they don't believe that it's fair for them to raise their prices.

Meanwhile they're cleaning windows inside of 10,000 square foot mansions for customers who aren't even home because they're too busy on vacation in the Caribbean islands spending money eating steak and drinking wine laughing all the way to the bank.

So while your on a ladder inside of their gigantic house, dripping in sweat, cleaning windows, might I add, thinking your so important because you have the pass codes to their house.

Your customer is busy landing on a plane where there is a white sandy beach.

By no means do I mean take advantage of your customers or rip them off and if you think that.. then I feel sorry for you because you're just stuck in a poverty mindset.

What I'm saying is that no man is better than any other man. If another man can make a lot of money and live his dreams, then so can you.

There was a phenomenal study done by Brene Brown author of the Power of Vulnerability.
She interviewed a bunch of people. Rich, poor, black, white, Asian, all types. The only common denominator that could possibly come up with as to why some people were happy and wealthy while others were dirt poor and miserable came down to one thing.

The happy, wealthy, healthy people felt that they were worthy of being happy and wealthy and healthy and... the broke miserable people DID NOT believe that they were worthy of being happy, wealthy and healthy.

It's easy for me to say this now, but the cold hard truth is.... If your just getting started, then all profit is good profit.
It's when you got a crew of guys and a ton of overhead to support, that the seriousness of having high prices and a well oiled machine comes into play.
Keep in the front of your mind that as soon as possible, run your business "as if" you had all the overhead before the overhead hits your reality.

Note: Look up an entrepreneur by the name of Dan Kennedy. This guy is a phenomenal marketer, copywriter, salesman and author.

He really breaks down the thought process of the wealthy. I promise you his stuff is mind blowing.

Sometimes somebody will share something with us, but we are not ready for it. I understand. I commend you and congratulate you for getting this far into my book.

Chapter 11

Window Screens and Pricing

Here's the fun part.
Do you want to talk about a frustrating nightmare? Do you want to pull your hair out and bang your head against the wall? Do you want to spend the next three years of your life learning the hard way about every different type of screen there is out there?
Most fun of all. learning how all of these different screens are installed and removed in all of these different customers houses?

Then... Once you've you finally figured it all out now, now you have to deal with your workers going through the same exact torment!

I could rant about window screens for the rest of this book. But I'm going to keep it down to one chapter to be nice. You really don't know what you're getting yourself into do you?

Actually I heard in the UK that they don't even use window screens. But here in the United States window screens are almost on every damn window. "Come on Keith why are you complaining about screens so much"?

You will see soon enough, Unless you're a veteran and an expert in this business. Screens will be the end of you. lol.

This is going to be hard to explain without inviting you into an actual home, but here goes.

 Different window cleaning companies have different policies. Some window cleaners will take out all of the screens for their customers so they don't have to. Some window cleaning companies might make their customers sign a waiver claiming that "the window cleaner is not responsible if screens break during removal due to some of them already being broken before hand".

I know a window-cleaner who sends all of his customers an email along with verbal instructions that the customer must move all furniture away from windows, open all drapes, raise all blinds and remove all screens before the window cleaners arrive.

If the customer fails to do so, then there is a separate extra charge for moving furniture and $2 for removing and replacing each screen.

 Reason being, it's very common for a screen to be broken inside of the window before the window cleaner touches it.

 Therefore if the customer removes the screen and it breaks, then it's the customer's fault.

 If the window cleaner removes the screen and it breaks, then there's no way to prove to the customer that it was already broken, so the fault falls on the window cleaner.

It takes some serious belief in yourself and your business to instruct your customer to move all furniture away from windows and remove all screens before arrival.

Note: *if you instruct your customer to do this make sure you give them at least a 24-hour advance notice.*
If your customer is late for a personal event or doesn't have the time to move furniture and screens away from window and

you tell them at the last minute. They're going to be extremely pissed off and never call you back.

I've experienced this personally because one of my customers who hired us was busy at work while his pregnant wife, at home taking care children was supposed to let us inside the home.

That morning on our way to the job I said to myself.

"Oh shoot. I forgot our new policy.
To tell the customer that they have to open all curtains, raise all blinds and remove all screens before we get there".

So... With no advance notice. I sent the customer a quick text message to remind him.
He instantly messaged me back, very frustrated and pissed off.

"Well if you would have told me this before I left for work this morning. Then I could have done it myself,   because I'm not going to call my pregnant wife, whose busy at home taking care of our children and tell her that she quickly has to rush around moving heavy dressers and furniture before you guys get there".

I quickly apologized and told him not to worry about it, that we would take care of it.
But that doesn't change the fact that my company pissed him off and
disrespected his time and family.

He may never call us back. Lesson learned.

Removing screens

When removing screens it's always best to carry tools. A couple different size flat-head screwdrivers should be all that you need. To be honest. On my belt loop everyday I carry a military grade foldable pocket knife. This thing works perfect for removing stubborn screens.

I could write an entire book about screens but you're going to have to learn this for yourself. a golden rule is to never force a screen in or out of a window track. but that's not true. sometimes you have to use gentle force and jiggle the screen back and forth in order to coax it out of position.

 This is something that takes time and finesse. If you ever break a customer screen, be honest and fix it out-of-pocket. If the customer finds out that you lied to them. They will never call you back.

Pricing Screen Cleaning

There are many ways to clean screens. With that being said, there are many ways to price screen cleaning. If you're only wiping down the screens with a dry towel then $2 per screen is fair. If you're only dusting the screens with a brush head Duster then $1 to $2 per screen is fair.

If the screens are filthy, and you're the one removing them and putting them back, then $3 per screen is fair.

 There are fancy screen cleaning machines that hook up to the customer's water spigot outside. The screen cleaning unit has water jets and bristle brushes that they're really wash the screens like a full-contact car wash. for something like this I would charge 3 to $4 per screen.

How to Clean Screens

Like I said. There are a lot of different screen styles and several ways to clean screens.
 if the screens are not too dirty then you can clean them right there in front of the window from which they came. This saves a lot of time from running around the house like a maniac Gathering up all of the screens and putting them outside on the front porch, or in the customer's garage.

 If the screens are really dirty then you're going to have to gather them up and take them outside before cleaning.
The problem with this is that now, you have 25 screens and don't know which screens go where. Now you're running around the house trying to find out how to put them back in like puzzle pieces.

Although there are solutions to this dilemma, it's also annoying and time-consuming. Like I said, if you can, clean the screen right in front of the customers window and put it back in.

 That being said… You can dry clean screens with a dry towel by wiping the screen down thoroughly in front and back. Then gripping and scrubbing the towel around the square frame.

You can also take a dry bristle duster and thoroughly dust the screen front and back.

Do not ever put a wet towel or scrubber onto a dirty screen unless you are planning on scrubbing it thoroughly. An hour after you leave the screens will try and look dirty again.

Screen Magic Product

There is an awesome product called screen Magic. It would compare to armor-all for the wet-look on car tires. This stuff when applied during screen cleaning makes the screens look shiny and black as if they were brand new. I'm telling you this stuff is awesome, but it's expensive, like $10 a bottle. I've heard of guys using armor-all but I'm not sure how good that stuff works.

You can offer screen magic to your customers and charge them an extra $0.25 per screen in order to pay for your product.

If you want to order screen magic go to www.DetroitSponge.com , ask for Mike and tell them Keith from YouTube sent you.

I also have an entire window cleaning starter kit called the "Keith Kit" at Detroit Sponge.

Call the number on their website and they'll hook you up.

Chapter 12

The Water Fed Pole

I have no doubt that this is going to be your favorite part of the book.
Why? Because the water fed Pole, in my opinion will become the most profitable tool in your new window cleaning business.

Disclaimer

Before reading this section, I want to disclose that the window cleaning business is a very diverse and multi perspective business when it comes to what tools one should use.
The water fed pole system is currently at Its pinnacle of window cleaning technology.
I do not claim to be an expert or authority about any of my claims in this section.
There are so many different ways to clean windows.

My way is probably not the best. So do not take my advice as gold.
Do your own research and find out what works best for you.
I will not be held responsible at the helm of other professional window cleaners
Due to inaccurate information or you arguing that my claims are true.

I have no doubt that this is going to be your favorite part of the book.
Why? Because the water fed Pole, in my opinion will become the most profitable tool in your new window cleaning business.

I could honestly write an entire book about the water fed pole system. There is so much more to it than meets the eye. I know you know me. So I'm going to start off with all the important how to stuff and pricing first. Then I'll share with you with my personal story about my first experience with the water fed pole system.

You can buy a complete truck or van Mount water fed pole system online or travel across the country and buy one. You can spend over $30,000 on a complete multi-stage water filtration system with an on-board water tank, batteries, power inverters, pumps, hoses, reels and all different size Carbon fiber and fiberglass poles.

I didn't have any start-up money personally. So I went to Detroit Sponge and got a basic bare bones system for $1,250. To the best of my knowledge, cleaning windows with a water fed pole system should be priced exactly the same as if you were climbing the ladder and doing it by hand with a squeegee. Just because it's easier and faster, by no means does that mean that you should charge less. That's why it cost more than a squeegee. And that's the whole point of technology. It's to make you more money in less time.

I use the water fed pole system on residential homes 90% of the time because an available water spigot is always on site. When it comes to cleaning storefronts and plazas, very rarely do you have available water, so you'll have to clean the windows by hand.

For small windows, I charge $3 medium size windows $4 large windows 5,6,7 even $16.
  or an extremely large window that's four times the size of a regular size window, that you would count as 4 Windows. When cleaning the windows with a standard basic water fed pole system. You want to hook up a standard contractor grade garden hose to the customer's water spigot on the side of their house. The reason I suggest using contractor grade garden hose is because it's thicker, more durable, doesn't kink or knot and allows more water volume to flow through the hose faster than standard or even cheaper garden hoses.

The hose hooks up to the first stage pre filter. Which is best designed to take out large sediments such as rust and sedimentary deposits that might be present in the water. The water flows from the first stage over to the second stage carbon filter which filters out lead deposits and any micro organisms in the water.

The third stage of the water filter is a carbon block filter which filters out almost everything except for the minerals in the water. I don't claim to know the exact science behind all of this, but I know it works.
  The next step in the water fed pole system can you go multiple ways.
You can now run your three stage purified water through a reverse osmosis filter.

A reverse osmosis filter is a membrane that is rolled up and housed inside of an aluminum metal or plastic tubular housing with water fittings on the end.
The bigger the reverse osmosis filter, the more water allowed to travel through it.

A reverse osmosis filter creates the same result as a water distillation chamber.

The distilled water process happens when you boil water inside of a chamber and lets the steam from that water transfer into a different chamber where it then settles and turns back into a liquid.

The water distillation process boils out impurities and the steam contains pure water.
If you have ever drank distilled water, it tastes completely flat.

A reverse osmosis filter creates a similar result, without having to have the complexities of a water distillation system.

Water must be completely filtered before going to an R/O filter because the membranes inside of the reverse osmosis filter are so tiny and small that they only allow the molecules of H_2O to pass through them. If you run direct tap water through a reverse osmosis membrane, you will probably dirty up and destroy that expensive filter within the matter of a couple window cleaning jobs.

This is the reason for a multi-stage filtration process. One filter takes out the big stuff. The next filter takes out the smaller stuff. The next filter takes out that even smaller stuff. And the reverse osmosis filter now takes out literally everything except for some left over microscopic minerals on the table of elements. I would like to mention that a reverse osmosis filter is not absolutely necessary in a water fed pole system.
And while we're on this topic, neither is a 3 stage water filter either.

In fact you can run dirty tap water from a customer's spigot, directly through the D/I resin tank and It will come out completely pure, containing 0.00% total dissolved solids.

Pure clean water, or as in the medical field they call it "hungry water", or "deionized water", Because it literally sucks and absorbs nearby minerals and dirt particles from its surrounding environment. It has negatively charged ions that are hungry to become rebalanced.

The bronze resin silica beads inside of the DI tank have negatively charged ions that literally suck and magnetically make minerals in the water stick to it like a super filter, that in the process, the molecules of pure H2O are the only liquid exiting the DI resin filter.

Although this is a very cheap option to get started. I would not recommend using a water fed pole system with only a DI tank hooked up to a water supply.
Reason being, DI resin is very expensive and you will be running through it very quickly. Therefore your price per gallon of water will be very expensive because you will have to replace the DI resin in your tank more frequently.

This is the reason for a pre-filter, sedimentary filter, carbon filter, carbon block filter and reverse osmosis filter are necessary before the DI filter.

This is where you hear the stories about RO/DI. It means that filtered water is running through a reverse osmosis filtration system and then being deionized through a DI tank. The reason an RO system is so expensive is because in almost all cases the city water pressure is nowhere near high enough to force the water through the microscopic membranes of the reverse osmosis system to allow enough pressure to come out of the Jets to clean the windows.

If you don't put at least a "100 PSI or 350 gallons per day" electronic pump in line between the water filters to force the water through. The the water product will just drizzle on to the windows and not be effective. You can buy a professional pump online or you can buy a cheap one at Harbor Freight and wire it all up yourself. This will take some experimentation and testing and probably some frustration to get it correct but you can also look online and on YouTube and see tons of examples where guys have created their own reverse osmosis systems with electronic pumps that shoot water out of their water fed pole systems.

In some cases I've seen window cleaners use multiple pumps or variable electronic pump systems Up to 300 PSI or more that create enough pressure to split the line and use two water fed poles at once.
This is freaking awesome but it's also expensive and takes time to get to that point.

When you run a water fed pole system through a multi-stage filtration process like the one described above. Your price of water per gallon become so extremely low and inexpensive that your expenses become almost non-existent, because all you're ever finding yourself replacing are the pre filters on your system.

Now if you're cleaning hundreds of Windows and doing hundreds of jobs a month.
 Then of course you're going to replace the reverse osmosis and Di filters more frequently, but dramatically less than compared to not having all these pre filters in place.

I hope all this make sense to you. You can look up all the stuff online and watch hours of videos on it on YouTube and read about it in a magazine articles and online forms such as the window cleaning resource.

But studying pure water technology is an absolute must if you want to understand why the water fed pole system that works the way it does.

Because if a customer asks you one day and you're not properly educated. Then you won't have any qualified answers to backup your claims as to why this thing actually works and why it works better than ladders and squeegees.

Next. Is a very important tool... Just like an electrician would use a Multimeter or a light tester. Professional window cleaners use something called a TDS meter or a total dissolved solids meter. This is something similar to a thermometer that you would stick in your mouth to measure a fever but instead it has two metal diodes at the end that you stick inside of the pure water coming out of the end of your water fed pole. It measures the amount of total dissolved solids in your water product in parts per million.

The exact specifications vary according to who you ask, but anything over 15 to 20 parts per million is bad because it shows that minerals are still existent in your water and will leave spots all over the glass. Perfectly clean pure water through this technology should always show up at 0.00 parts per million. and you should also test you are water product at every single job or at least and every single different city because different cities have different levels of minerals present in their tap water. Also the reason to carry a total dissolved solids meter on your truck or van is to test the water frequently to let you know and gage when is the right time to replace the filters in your system.

NEXT

Note: Partly, what makes windows dirty are minerals from rain water built up on the glass. In severe cases they create what is called "hard water mineral stains".
Even though you can clean glass with tap water solution and a squeegee. A squeegee still wipes all of the water off of the glass. So the result is a spot free window.
On the other hand. The water fed pole is different because there is no squeegee to wipe off the glass. The glass has to dry "spot free". If you use tap water with a water fed pole system the result would leave a hazy, milky film of minerals all over the windows.
That's why the water fed pole system requires "super filtered mineral free water", Because it leaves the windows spot-free. Similar to the spot-free rinse at a carwash.

I would like to tell you about the time when I was so embarrassed after we left a customer's house. I was so proud after doing a great job cleaning their windows with the water fed pole system. Only to get a call a couple hours later that every single window on their house looked like somebody had splashed hazy milk all over the windows.

We had to come back and clean the entire house for free because I wasn't aware that the DI tank had used up its resin and now was spitting dirty mineral filled water all over the customer's windows.

I don't want you to make the same mistake. So test your water with a TDS (total dissolved solids)"Around $20 at DetroitSponge.com" meter to make sure the water is always within the proper Purity levels. So you can leave your customers and their windows with a great end result.

Now for the actual water fed poles. You can get all different types of poles made by every single major window cleaning brand from Ettore, to Unger, and many more.

They start out from as small as 15 feet and go all the way up to 85 and possibly even 115 feet.

I'm not kidding, guys it literally have a spotter stand next to them with a pair of binoculars, or they wear binoculars themselves while operating these insane window cleaning contraptions.

The water fed poles are made out of fiberglass or carbon fiber materials which are extremely light, flexible and easy to maneuver. There are different levels of telescoping chambers and collars that make the water fed pole system work by allowing it to collapse in on itself in a tubular fashion. Then as you extend the poles, one by one.

They telescope all the way up to the sky and lock into place with locking fastener collars.

Running From the DI tank all the way to end through the middle of the water fed pole, is a long rubber tube that carries the water all the way to the top where it exits out of the gooseneck and brush. Hence; the water fed Pole.

Then the water travels through a splitter and exit out of two Jets that shoot water from inside of the brush head and onto the glass. In my experience, if the water pressure in the city you are working in is not very high. Then you cannot extend the water fed pole more than 15 feet because the upward gravity pressure increases, similar to water being pumped up a skyscraper for the tenants inside.

Without enough water pressure the water will just dribble out of the pole.
In most cases, the water pressure is high enough for you to extend all the way up to 35 feet without an issue. But once you get into water fed poles that are 45, 55, 65, 75, 85 feet. You definitely need to start buying and installing pumps in order to force the water to shoot out of the Jets with enough pressure in order to rinse the glass off more efficiently and faster.

Does this all makes sense to you? See, you can get started with a water fed pole very cheaply for about $1,200 bucks. That's $650 for the pole and brush and another couple hundred dollars for all the tubing and attachments. About $400 more for the DI tank and a basic dolly to strap it to. Now with your mobile water fed pole system you can pull it out of your truck, van or trailer and wheel it right over to your customers spigot and hook it up with a garden hose.

Then have a 150 foot water tube line go from the DI tank all the way to the pole.
This allows you to walk around a customer's entire house without having to move the tank...so you can clean the windows efficiently.

When you get into cleaning homes or commercial buildings that are over two stories.

You will need to start investing more money and finding ways to filter the water better so you can reach higher than you did before.

How to use the water fed pole system

Using the water fed Pole is actually pretty easy. Kind of hard to describe in a book, but I will try. You want to scrub the windows up and down at every single possible angle. Starting at the top and bottom sections of the windows where minerals usually build up.
I personally like to not only scrub from top to bottom. But I also scrub from left to right, as well to make sure I'm getting every square inch of the window.

Each window should take anywhere from 60 to 90 seconds. I like to make sure that the brush goes up and down the same area of glass at least 6 passes before I move the brush over. So I know and see that the window is getting thoroughly scrubbed.

Once you know that that window was thoroughly scrubbed. Pull the brush away from the window and let the jets rinse the window thoroughly. Sweeping from left to right very slowly. Let the Jets create a sheet of water that runs down the glass like a waterfall.

If you see the water parting on a little speck. That means there is still dirt or a particle stuck to the glass. Rescrub that area. Once again, sweep the water from left to right gently. Make sure that you do not get the water above the window on any plastic, vinyl or window frames, because that will mix with any dirt that's on any vinyl siding or sills above the window.

 Because after you rinse the window down... water mixed with dirt will drip back down the window and leave dirty drip lines. This takes some practice in the beginning. To isolate your work area so you scrub and rinse only the glass itself.

Obviously, you cannot stop gravity causing water to run below the window.
So you should always start from top to bottom. When you're done scrubbing and rinsing all of the windows, they take about 15 minutes to dry.

They will dry spot free like a spot free car wash. After the windows dry, walk around the property and check for spots or drips. If you indeed find drips. re clean and re rinse those windows. Once you get super proficient with the water fed pole system. You'll notice more and more that you never have to go back to touch up
The windows.

Once you get really good with the water fed pole system. You can clean the entire outside of mansions in like 45 minutes and make buku bucks.

So I hope you get started with the best possible water fed pole system that you can afford.
I personally use the **Ettore Aquaclean** 35 foot reach with a basic di tank.
Then I went on eBay and spent a hundred bucks on a three-stage under the sink water filtration system.

By the time you're reading this book. I probably will have invested in a reverse osmosis system with pumps and the whole nine yards. In time, I hope you will too and I hope you're very excited about getting your new water fed pole system. This thing is the future of window cleaning.

Now let me tell you my story about the water fed Pole. But before I do, I want to remind you of one more thing. Yes you can create your own water fed pole system out of miscellaneous parts and do it yourself. Yes it will be cheaper. But I promise you you will be running around hardware and department stores like Home Depot and Lowe's pulling your freaking hair out frustrated... going back and forth... trying to get all of the correct tools, fittings and parts necessary to make your new insane Einstein Contraption work.

I'm warning you in advance so you don't pull your hair out and say I didn't warn you.
haha.
Just like learning anything new, the water fed pole system could drive you crazy when first getting started. It's all part of the game.

Now here's my story of the water fed pole system.

It was freezing winter and I was going into my second season cleaning windows. I had climbed up and down ladders as if the water fed pole was never even invented. I'm not afraid of heights, but I hate ladders. To make money in the window cleaning business, you have to get used to climbing on ladders.

I'll tell you. I tried cheating the system by getting 20 foot long extension poles and trying to clean two story windows from the ground. Yeah, doesn't work very well. So I thought I was doomed to climbing ladders. Then I saw a YouTube video of the water fed pole system. I got a feeling in my gut so strong, it was a feeling of certainty. Even though I was flat broke, I knew for a fact that this piece of equipment would change the destiny of my window cleaning business.

As soon as my wife got home. I showed her the video and excitedly told her that I would buy a water fed pole for our company this spring. Knowing we were behind on the bills, She detested and was very upset that I would be blowing money on something so expensive. But I knew for a fact, no matter what, even if I had to dump out change, I would get a water fed pole system.

A month later we were on a window cleaning job. This was the most difficult client we have and his windows are over 28 feet high and almost impossible to clean without risking your life. I left the job site and drove directly to Detroit Sponge here in Wixom Michigan. When I met the owner Mike. I told him that I was broke and needed to get started with the cheapest water fed pole system possible.

He showed me around and one hour later I walked out with the Ettore Aqua Clean 35ft. reach Water Fed Pole and a Basic Large DI Tank.

I'll explain more about the science behind the water fed Pole later on in the chapter.

When I arrived at my wealthy clients house. I set up the water fed pole and started practicing what I had seen in the Youtube videos by scrubbing the windows and letting the water jets rinse off the glass.

I was so excited. But my excitement turned to nervous frustration when my client came out and started watching me clean his windows. He immediately started questioning the water fed Pole and wanted to know why I wasn't cleaning the windows like usual with a scrubber, squeegee and Ladders.

I didn't want to tell him that I was terrified and stressed out from cleaning his high up two-story windows by hand.

These are not ordinary two-story windows, I promise you if you saw this house you would know why. You literally have to stand at the top rung of the ladder and then a hold on with your fingertips to the side of the house while leaning back. It's a death-defying Act.

I told him that my new window cleaning system actually worked better than the squeegee.

He called my bluff and told me that he doesn't want me using it and he doesn't like it. he started pointing out little microscopic spots on the windows and accusing me of doing poor quality work, being lazy and trying to rip him off by buying a low-quality scam artist-made piece of equipment. He told me that "the product is shit", that it didn't work and that I got ripped off because the only way to clean windows is with the scrubber and squeegee.

By this time I was in total anxiety. I buckled to my customers wishes, put away the water fed Pole and continued cleaning windows on the ladder with a scrubber and squeegee. An hour later my customer left and that's when I brought the water fed pole back out and continued to clean his windows MY WAY!

By the time we got around to the back of the house. I had taught my worker how to use the water fed pole so I could go ahead and start cleaning the inside of the house.

When I walked in the front room. I saw water running all down his walls and all over his extremely expensive mahogany wood floors. I panicked and ran to get handfuls of towels and started soaking the water up while yelling "stop stop" out an adjacent window.

It was then that I realized that the seals and gaskets were blown on his windows.

I quickly cleaned up the mess and it wasn't a big deal. but when I looked up, to my surprise, the windows looked absolutely gorgeous. Gigantic plate glass windows sparkling in the sunshine. My customer didn't have a clue. I wish I could say that now every single job was a water fed pole job, but that wasn't the case.

The truth is. I actually questioned myself whether or not the water fed pole really did work as good as a scrubber and squeegee? I stressed out so bad because for some reason, deep down inside I felt like a part of me was lying and ripping off my customers.

Even though back then my prices were so low that It was completely ridiculous anyways. I couldn't believe that cleaning windows went from being so hard and scary, to being so fun and easy. I couldn't believe that I was making $200 to clean a house in 2 hours and the ladders never even left the truck.

I don't know about you, but I grew up completely brainwashed and was lied to that the secret to becoming successful is hard

work. I actually believed that if the job was physically easy, then I must be doing something wrong.
I actually believed that
because I'd been stuck in shitty dead end jobs for the past 15 years. That I must work my guts out to make a living.

Basically, I was so insecure about the water fed pole that my own customers started questioning me and questioning the quality of the system. To make matters worse. Not only did I attract negative attention to the water fed pole, but I also openly offering my customers too much scientific jargon and making excuses of how It's actually better than a squeegee.

This is insane what I'm about to tell you. but I created a scenario. I literally manifested a perception that made my customers instantly not like my new fancy water fed pole system.

Dude, I'm telling you if you have the best product in the world but you have no confidence in yourself or your product. Then no one else will have confidence in you or your product either. It's so easy for someone to tell you that you have to have more confidence. But if you've never done a thing, if you've never tried a thing, and you don't even understand the way it really works. Then how in the hell are you supposed to have confidence if you don't know 100% for sure if the product really actually is what it claims to be??

I asked myself. *"Can the water fed pole system could scrub an extremely dirty, 2 story window the way a microfiber scrubber and persons physical arm strength can?"*

This caused a moral dilemma for me and a ton of moral anxiety. I felt like I was lying to my customers because I was secretly being lazy and sick and tired of climbing ladders.

It took some time to get rid of this weird poverty, guilt-minded mentality.
That's why I teach in the form of stories. Because deep down, you might share these same self-limiting beliefs.
But not for long!

Chapter 13

Window Cleaning Tools

1.) Squeegees
2.) Scrubbers
3.) Tool Belt
4.) Razor blades (Designed for window cleaners)
5.) Dusters
6.) Ladders (My favorite is the multi-position 22 foot Werner from Home Depot $189)
7.) Extension poles
8.) Towels
9.) Solution (Cheap DIY Dawn & Vinegar (1 Tablespoon per gallon water and 1 shot glass of vinegar)
10.) Water-fed Pole System
11.) Plastic Shoe Covers (*Always wear inside customers homes no matter what*)
12.) Blue Huck surgical towels and
13.) Microfiber towels
14.) Generic spray bottles
15.) Pressurized spray bottles
16.) Large rolling tote bins
17.) Ostrich feather dusters
18.) Ceiling fan dusters
19.) Contractor garden hose
20.) Garden hose jet nozzles
21.) Assorted brushes for dust and cobwebs
22.) A banjo to play, so you can entertain your customers in their living rooms.

My Favorite Brands

In my business I personally use all

a.) Sorbo squeegees.
b.) Pulex side holster buckets,
c.) Unger window cleaning belts with extra Loops for holding towels
d.) Unger blue and aluminum extension poles (every size available small to large)
e.) Glass Gleam 4 Window cleaning solution from www.DetroitSponge.com
  (*Tell them Keith from YouTube sent you and ask about the "Keith Kit"*)

The truth is, don't take my word as gold. there are several different brands that people swear by. I have used several of them, but once I tried Sorbo squeegees for instance. I fell in love.
The top name-brand squeegee, after 100 hours of use will begin to feel like an extension of your hand.

 After doing anything long enough you develop what is called, sensory acuity. But don't underestimate the power of becoming friends with other window cleaners, finding a mentor and even watching YouTube videos in order to learn better techniques.

Everything you could ever need is at

Detroit Sponge
1-800-535-6394
Detroit Sponge & Chamois
48050 West Rd. Wixom MI. 48393
www.DetroitSponge.com

They deliver all over the United States.
If you're outside of the United States, check your local
supplier.

Mike Waroway
1-800-535-6394
Detroit Sponge & Chamois
48050 West Rd. Wixom MI. 48393
www.DetroitSponge.com

Also WCRA
www.WindowCleaningResource.com

And
J.C Racenstein

How to Clean Windows

Along with this book there's an entire video training course
called The Window Cleaning Blueprint.
I hope that you pick up a copy for yourself at

Although this book is jam packed with information. The *Separately Sold* video course is priceless and will create a fast track to your success in this business.+

Chapter 14

How to Go Legit and Pay Taxes

DISCLAIMER

Although I happen to run my own legitimate business and pay my own taxes.
I am not professional Tax Advisor or certified public accountant.
Do not take my words as gold because they're nothing more than opinion.
Consult your own Tax Advisor, do things by the book and always pay your taxes.

"So you know I'm telling the truth. In this section I'll share my own story"

In a perfect world you're supposed to have all of your ducks in a row before collecting a single dollar.
However, when I first got started in the window cleaning business..
I lost everything I owned. I was flat broke, having panic attacks and coming home to an eviction notice.

On top of trying to learn how to run a business. You will be faced with so many challenges that it could drive you into having a personal meltdown.

Back in the day, I learned valuable business lessons the hard way.
I found myself scrambling in anxiety and raising all my prices on my customers in order to pay for proper insurance and taxes.

My prices were way too low because I wasn't confident in my work, I wasn't confident in myself, I knew nothing about the window cleaning business, knew nothing about business finance and didn't know how to even run a small business

The truth was I was terrified that if I went legit too early, I would create all of these new bills that I couldn't afford and worst of all I was afraid that the work would stop coming in and I would be totally screwed.

I went legit at the end of my first full season and showed all of my business income.
To my amazement I was able to write off a lot of my expenses and pay very little in taxes.

I also learned that getting Insurance wasn't as expensive as I had dreaded. At least in Michigan a general liability insurance policy it's somewhere around $1,000 year. That's less than $100 a month.

trust me, not having insurance will stop you from getting higher-paying jobs. On the contrary having insurance will get you higher-paying jobs and more money. You have to trust me on this.
If you're already starving in the desert and somebody asks you for a cup of water, that can be pretty stressful.

If you're walking across the desert hoping there will be water on the other side, that can be stressful too.
Obviously there are no guarantees but the guarantees you make for yourself.

If you have these fears, you're not alone. These are common small business fears.
Getting on the ball, getting serious and learning everything you possibly can about running a small business will protect you because knowledge is power.

In your window cleaning business, just like any business.
Going legit is not a should,
but a must. Why? Here's why.
If you or one of your workers goes to clean a window "and that window already has a crack in it", what happens if that window accidentally breaks?
What if it's a $10,000 eyelid window above a customer's front door?
One mistake like that could put you out of business.

Here's another example. What if you are customers like to pay you by check? Are you going to sleep at night knowing you're cashing checks through your personal bank account? Bottom line is. if you're afraid of going legit, it's probably because your prices will be too low in the beginning.

If this is your first business and nobody ever took you by the hand and showed you how to run a legitimate business, then it's not your fault. But, it is your responsibility to learn the ropes as quickly as possible.
 Because one day if the hammer drops on you. There will be nobody there to save you.
And it certainly will be entirely your fault.

There's a saying that is very true.
 "Operate your business as if these things were already true".

Operate your business as if you were legit, before even being legit. So when you actually go legit, you already have the money to pay for it

 When you decided to go fully legit... without raising my prices way beforehand.
 It will be much too late, and you'll be on window cleaning jobs having anxiety attacks Because you are working for free and are terrified of asking the customer for more money.

 You want to talk about a catch 22 question?

There's no worst fear in small business, left feeling of running out of money faster than you can make it. the feeling of hopelessness. the feeling of discouragement. I've been there. & I don't want you to be there. If you're there, I want you to get out of it to become successful as fast as possible.

You can register your small business by going in any of these several routes.

    1.) www.sba.gov.

    2.) www.Legalzoom.com

    3.) find a small business accountant or CPA and pay him/her to get your paperwork started.

Back to SBA.gov

    4.) On Www.sba.gov *Locate your state.*

"If you live outside of the United States, I'm sorry I don't know the website but I'm sure there's something similar or whatever country you live in".

    2.)Find the link called "register your business name". Walk through the steps,
fill out all of your personal and new business information and get your EIN taxpayer ID number.
 choose LLC, S Corp, or DBA.

I'm not going to go and to the differences between these entities here,
but you can get an amazing book by Robert Kiyosaki's Advisors called "Own your own Corporation",
on ebook or audiobook. This book as well as many other audiobooks change my life.

3.) pay the fee.

4.) A couple weeks later you will get paperwork in the mail from the IRS stating that you have a new business and EIN number.

5.) Take that paperwork in to your local bank or credit union and start a new small business checking and savings account.

6.) Bam! You're in business.

7.) Ask around for anyone you know of that runs a small business. Even if it's the guy who runs the auto care center down the street. Keep asking around for anybody who knows a CPA who specializes in helping small business owners.

8.) Once you find an accountant. Bring him coffee and happily pay him.
Stay in touch with your accountant quarterly and have him set you up on regular tax payments. Also, bring your accountant a list of questions for him to answer every time.

If you're just filing and paying taxes but not learning anything in the process, that's just plain stupid.

One more thing about owning a new small business.

This means that you've created a new living entity " corporation" And that you are responsible for filing a tax return for that Corporation at least every calendar year.

A corporation has its own social security.number EIN number and is now a living entity that operates separately from your social security number.

I could get very deep into all this stuff but I will not for the sake of this book.

GETTING INSURED

Getting general liability insurance is incredibly easy and cheap.   you should expect to pay around $1,000 a year for a simple small business. if you're on a payment plan it's less than $100 a month.
Contact your auto insurance provider or whoever insurse your vehicle and ask them if they offer small business insurance plans.

 This is presuming that you already have a car or truck and have Auto Insurance.
In my opinion.
The most critical form of insurance you can have is Automotive coverage.
If by chance you're operating a small business and driving around with no vehicle insurance and you get into an accident. You could be sued for everything you have and your future for many years to come.
As far as I'm aware it's illegal not to have automobile insurance anyways.

Anyways, look up local insurance companies or insurance agents on Google maps.
It's free for them to run the numbers and find out how cheaply you can get a bottom line policy.

 If you don't have the money right away. Go do a couple window cleaning jobs and then invest the money into general liability insurance. If by chance you're financially broke and terrified and reading this. You can still go around on foot cleaning storefronts, strip malls and plazas and get some regular window cleaning accounts underneath your belt.

Then in the near future go out and get proper insurance.

To finish off this section. there are a lot of amazing ebooks and audiobooks that go into great detail about setting up and running small businesses.
These books will change your life for the better I promise you.

Some of my favorite Books and authors on these subjects are.

Tony Robbins
Suze Orman
Robert Kiyosaki
John Jantsch
Small Business for Dummies
Tax Free Wealth - Kiyosaki's Advisor's
Lower Your Taxes BIG TIME
Debt Cures by Kevin Trudeau
Accounting for Dummies

etc.

Chapter 15

The 30% Rule
For Tax Time - For Lifetime

The 30% rule. The 30% rule changed my life. One of my best friend's, Scotty here in Michigan went from broke to becoming a multimillionaire in his construction and real estate businesses.
By turn of events he lost a huge chunk of his business and is now on his way to being a millionaire again.

Scotty, my mentor taught me the rule of 30%.
He says,
"Put away 30% of all gross income and you will never have financial problems ever again".

You might say,
"WHAT? if I put away 30% I would be broke, I would lose everything.
I can't even afford to put away 10%"

 Haha, I know my first year That's what I used to say.
If your prices are too low then in a few years you will be out of business regardless.
So...Raise your prices in the very beginning of your business.
If you can't afford to put away 30% of all gross income, then immediately start tacking on 30 percent to all of your new quotes and customers.

Then go back to your existing customers, "If you already have them", and tell them you need to tack on at least 10% to their existing price.

Give them a long drawn-out story about, how In order to keep providing them with good reliable service you need to raise the price by 10%. Tell them you have taxes and insurance toupee. Tell them you want to grow a professional legitimate company so you can stick around and keep serving them years down the road.

If you keep blabbing and talking about it they'll say "okay, okay 10% is fine.":

Note: *While this approach may work for a self-employed One Man Show it may be an unprofessional approach for a larger company.*

Whatever it takes, get more money.

Use the split test to raise prices

If you want to make enough money to be able to put away 30% of all
gross income and grow a legitimate business.
Keep your personal thoughts and feelings out of it.
Because if you're afraid to raise your prices. that has zero to do with
your market or your marketplace. It has everything to do with you.

Once again.

Just to make sure you're paying attention because this is so important,
I have to mention it twice.
When in doubt, utilize the A/B split test. Split your leads down the middle.
It doesn't Necessarily have to be 50/50. But at some juncture, decide which percentage of your new leads and customers you will raise the price on.

So. half of them gets charged more. The other half stays the same.
If you're having trouble choosing which 50% of your new quotes to raise the price on.
Raise your price on the percentage of customers that live the nicer homes in the higher end neighborhoods.

One storefront you walk in to tell them $15. The other storefront you walk into
"same size, different city" tell them $25.

Split tests are used commonly in many places, especially marketing. Some marketers won't even put their stamp of approval on their literature until it has been proven to convert it's highest percentage through multiple split tests.

A marketing example would be putting out two advertisements in two different neighborhoods.
One that has the original standard price and the other ad that has a higher price.
One ad simply says one thing, while the other ad says another.

This way you are not stuck being one-track minded. Feeling like you have no other options is the way of the poor.

Successful people always try to ask themselves. "How can I have both"?

Use split tests whenever possible and don't forget it. Split tests are the best ways to raise prices with the lowest amount of risk.

I like split tests because they didn't occur to me when I started my window cleaning business. I was stuck banging my head against the wall charging everybody the same price. I had to learn about split testing and try it for myself to learn about its magic.

It's just so funny how the simplest things that can make us more profit, go right over our heads.

I understand that "you win some you lose some". But if you don't figure out how to put money away.
Then your dream of having a small business will turn into the worst nightmare you could have ever imagined.

The plain truth is that you need to figure out how to make more money faster.
That's like the stupidest thing I could have said here because it's so obvious.
But that is the same situation we're all in.

The sooner you learn how to drive a wedge between your income in expenses is the safer you'll be and better chance you'll have of realizing your dreams.

That means living as cheaply as possible, working with what you have and working your ass off to the bone in the meantime.

Saving 30% of all gross income will allow you to pay all of your taxes during tax time. After write-offs, whatever is leftover will be a bonus for you to reinvest back into your company or save for an emergency fund.

 If you're not making enough money to even pay the bills let alone save money, here are some small business & money tips
 The first step is becoming aware that you don't know what you don't know.
Realizing that you need to learn these things puts you at a great advantage.

 There are some amazing audiobooks on Audible.com that will educate you on the "ins & outs"
of small business while you're out cleaning windows.

Investing a small percentage of all of your income back into ongoing education will be the difference between being broke in 5 years or being financially successful.

If you can't put away 30% of your income below are some possible reasons why.

1.) **You need to learn more about marketing and advertising**. Get a book called "Guerrilla Marketing Tactics" by Jay Conrad Levinson. Also an amazing book called "Duct Tape Marketing by John Jantsch.

2.) **Your overhead is too high and you need to cut unnecessary expenses**. Get a book called Profit First by Mike Michalowicz _____

_____

3.) Need to raise prices Watch videos on Youtube and get books on wealth attraction and raising prices by Dan Kennedy. Also get Grant Cardone audiobook "Sell or Be Sold"

4.) Need more customers. Pick up a book called "The Referral Engine" by John Jantsch.

5.) Believe in yourself. Get an audio book called "The Answer" by John Assaraf.

Money flows to those who can organize their thoughts and orchestrate resources into sequences that create predictable results.
Keith Kalfas.

"When the time comes that the pain of changing is less painful than the pain of staying the same, you'll change"
Orrin Woodward

What I'm saying is when you can force yourself to sit down and write out specific plans & goals, then go out and execute those plans. That's when you come up with that extra 30%.

There are people who have overcome overwhelming odds and still became successful.
If they can do it, we can do it.

Work your guts out and learn this business inside and out until you are consistently saving 30% of all gross income. Do not increase your lifestyle and do not invest in fancy trucks or equipment only to make yourself look better. Only advance your business or take on loans on fancy equipment if you have big jobs or contracts lined up that require that fancy equipment in order to get the job done.

If you look fancy but I have no money in the bank account, then that's not fancy.

That's just plain stupid!

Chapter 16

Collecting Customer info and Booking jobs

Telephone Protocol

Requirements

a.) Contacts Gmail/ Email
b.) Google Calendar
c.) Have headset on and Phone out and ready to capture

    1.) Customers contact information,
    2.) Phone number
    3.) First and Last Name
    4.) Home Address
    5.) Email address
    6.) Where they Learned about our services
    7.) Possibly a note If the customer has odd or special requests
    8.) Sell Job Directly Over Phone and Book job
    9.) Book Quote

Note: *Everything in this chapter can also be accomplished with CRM tools.*
(customer relationship management) tools.

Infusionsoft
Service Autopilot
QuickBooks

Freshbooks
Quicken
and many more

Well not as advanced as the services listed above.
Google has cheap tools that works great for small businesses.

The CRM services list above are awesome because they integrate with your existing email, bookkeeping, customer database, tracking, billing and calendar platforms.

The great thing about a CRM is that you can run your entire business inside of one integrated product platform.
Okay, the number one thing that brings money in the door is marketing and advertising.
Why? Because marketing and advertising make the phone ring.
Once you've got that locked down.
Here's a simple process for handling inbound telephone calls.
Feel free to improvise as you wish.

 I even give you permission to copy this script into your phone and print it out.
 The more you practice the stuff the better you will get.

I personally wear a set of (LG HBS) bluetooth headphones while talking to customers
so I can type their information directly into my smartphone while providing me with contact information.
Once you get good at typing while talking, you'll also be able to insert quick notes about the customer as well.

I have an entire database of contact information, email addresses and notes about every customer I've ever done work for. Some people call this organized. I call it survival instincts.

Below is a telephone script. Feel free to use it when communicating with new customers.
 Every word in the script is designed with specific intention. Literally every word.

The prices may not match our Market period improvise the script to match your own business.
 also look up "National Window Cleaning Averages" on Google.

Pay Attention!

Residential Homes

a.) Read the script carefully because it goes in different directions.
b.) Always try to book the job over the phone and show up ready to work.
c.) It's smart to ask the customer to move furniture and knick-knacks away from Windows.
d.) It's smart to ask the customer to open all drapes and raise all blinds.
e.) it's smart to have the customer either verbally agree or sign a waiver that you are not responsible 4 broken blinds.

 You have no idea how many times one of my workers or myself went to pull the string to raise the blinds and the entire set of blinds fall off the wall in the customer's living room.

You have no idea how many times I went to take a screen out of a customer's window and the thing crumbled in my fingertips.

99% of people do not pay attention to the mechanics of their windows and blinds and shades until the day they hire a window cleaner. Now you show up and clean the windows, break a set of 50 year old blinds and now you're getting accused and have to pay for it.

Remember you are running a professional business. So arguing with a customer will only destroy your reputation and get you bad reviews on the internet. In the information age it is never been so vital to protect your business and your reputation by means of over communicating to your customers up front.

If you're just getting started in the window Cleaning business. Putting policies, procedures and paperwork together can feel like a daunting task. I'm not going to sit here and lie to you and tell you that I had all the stuff figured out in the beginning. I did not. I was it complete mess, running around in my customers homes and total anxiety over the possibility of the slightest accident.

My business coach would repeatedly advise me to put policies and procedures in place in order to protect my business. but when you are in fight or flight mode and battling for your own Survival. All you can think about is getting money so your life doesn't go down the drain.

In reality "Unless you come from college background or family of people who taught you how to document business practices". In the beginning.

1.) You won't know how to do this and it's not your fault.

2.) You don't have the money to hire an attorney to do it for you.

3.) You'll have to create these policies yourself or borrow them from someone else.

Most people have no idea how to even run their own small business, let alone draft up contracts, waivers, liability release forms and document systems .

Most small business owners don't put policies and procedures in place until they've repeatedly bang their head against the wall until the point of mental and emotional exhaustion.

A lot of this might not make sense to you right now. But trust me, it will.

Enough with my ranting.
Although I hope you enjoyed it, let's move on to the telephone script.

Remember, the script is only a script. In real life, the conversation can go many different ways.
The script is designed to close the sale.

If you want to get really deep into selling.
Pick up a book by Grant Cardone called The Closer's Survival Guide.

Window Cleaning Service
Telephone Script

You:
Hi, Thank you for calling <u>Your window cleaning service,</u>
this is <u>Your name</u> *speaking. How can I help you*?

Customer: "Yes, Bla Bla Bla"

No matter what the customer says next... You say

"Great!
From what **website** *did you learn about our services"?*
NOTE: *(If you say any other word but* **website***. the customer will say, "The internet"... Then you end up asking them the same damn question in the first place.)*

Customer: Oh from Craigslist, Google, Yelp Etc.
<u>Record that info</u>

You: Fantastic! How can I help you today?

Customer: *I was looking to have my windows cleaned and I was looking to have my windows* cleaned and I was wondering how much you charge for window cleaning?

You: "Ok, we have 3 different Service packages.

First we have what we call our basic package…
and that's Glass cleaning outside only at $5 per window pane"

Second "we have our deluxe package...
That's glass cleaning outside and inside,
at $7 per window
We also offer screen cleaning at $2 per screen"

"And finally we have our **Premium package**
Which is also our most expensive package.
That includes glass cleaning inside and out,
plus Tracks and Sills wiped down
and all screens cleaned.
And that runs $10 per window"

How soon were you looking to have them cleaned?

Customer: "Right Away"

You: *Okay we have to 2 times available. This Thursday morning between 8:30 - 9:00 a.m... or Friday afternoon between 2 and 3 p.m.*

Do either of these work for you?

Customer: *"Friday afternoon is perfect!"*

YOU: *"Great! what's your email address so we can send you a confirmation?"* **_then collect data and book job_**

(Optional) **YOU:** *Please move any furniture and knick-knacks away from the windows. Please open all drapes and lift up all blinds before we arrive.*

Customer: *"Well, can you give me a round about price so I know how much is going to cost?"*

You:
"Sure, we have two different ways that we give quotes.

   1.) We can provide you an instant quote if you

just email us 4 pictures of your home.
Front, back, left, and right.
2.) Or we can come out and leave you a Quote on paper.
Which do you prefer"?

Customer: *You can just come and leave a quote on my front door.*

You: *"Great, do you still want to lock Friday afternoon in?"*

Customer: *Yes but I want a quote first*

You: *Great we have GPS navigation.*
All I need is your address city, zip, First & Last Name
NOTE: *(If you don't tell the customer you have GPS navigation. they might go on blabbing for*
20 minutes, giving you turn-by-turn directions to their house like it was 1994.)

Customer: Gives you information

You: *"Great! Will be there within 24 hours. You can expect to see a quote on your front door,*

But we're booked out and can't lock down the date for cleaning without confirmation.

So call us or send us a quick email as soon as you get the quote and we'll get you on the schedule and get your windows cleaned... Okay?"

Customer: ok

Follow Up

And of course follow up with a customer
in no less than 48 hours and say...

YOU: *"Hello, this is _____ with <u>window cleaning service</u>. We stopped by Thursday and gave you a quote for cleaning your windows inside and out for $225."*

"Would you like to go ahead and get that done? "

The No Brainer Close

We can take 10% off your bill and do the job for $200 and we'll even throw in Free Screen Cleaning Service if you book a cleaning with us today.

Would you like to go ahead and get on our schedule?

Customer: *Well, I might have been born in a barn, but I'm definitely not stupid Enough to pass up a deal like this…*

see you Thursday Fools!

$$$$$

End Script

Chapter 17

Your Systems

Administrative tasks

Aside from running around like a maniac cleaning windows all day.
There's various things you have to do behind the scenes to keep a business running smoothly.

Below are some notes of literally exactly what I do in my very own window cleaning business.

In the future, it would be optimal to have a secretary do all this stuff.

1. First thing every single morning,
   Renew between 1 and 3 craigslist ads
   on one account.

2. One ad for residential window cleaning.
3. One ad for commercial/ storefronts.

4. At lunch time renew 1 to 3 more ads on a different
   Craigslist accounts.   *(With different emails)*

5. in the afternoon before getting off work, renew 1 to 3 more craigslist ads on a third email account

6. Every morning check voicemails, return calls, follow up with customers.
7. Check email to follow up with customers and send over quotes.
8. login to yodle and signpost (Marketing CRM's)to follow up with leads.   Place ads on Facebook, newspapers, Google ads, and general marketing.

9. Answer phone calls, schedule quotes, send out invoices and estimates. Collect money, pickup checks, cash, Swipe credit cards
10. Make Bank Deposits, pay bills and order checks.

11. Log into QuickBooks, manage bookkeeping, accounting, payroll.

12. Go out in the field, do property walks and give quotes to customers.
13. Manage social media, share posts, graphics coupons, discounts, Facebook, Google+ and place Facebook ads.
14. Manage online vendors including ordering marketing materials from online vendors such as door hangers, business cards, refrigerator magnets, Flyers, www.Uprinting.com
15. Order paper carbon copies for Window Cleaning invoices and go pick them up. Etc. etc.
    Order bandit signs and go pick them up

16. Ordering t shirts, hats, apparel from Eagraphics.com, Communicate with art department.

17. Run errands and pick up, materials from Home Depot / Lowes.

18. Talk on the phone to all of these persistent marketing companies All over the country that try to sign you up for their services everyday.

.

19.) Updating search listings comma adding pictures of work being done to websites,   Facebook pages, Google my places for business.

Chapter 18

When Working On a Jobsite

Storefronts

This is going to be fun to explain in a book.
Rule of thumb would seem like taking the path of least resistance.
But I've learned a lot. Commercial window cleaning such as storefronts, plazas, liquor stores and restaurants are easy to learn. You just keep cleaning the next window. I like to go from right to left while simultaneously cleaning from top to bottom.

Obviously, always clean higher Windows first and wipe any possible drips off before they roll down so they don't get on Lower windows. On super dirty windows you have to use more solution and sometimes literally dunk the entire scrubber inside of your solution and slap it onto the windows. Sometimes windows are so dirty you have to literally clean them twice.

Wash, squeegee, repeat. "Charge Twice" If you get too much liquid on the Windows sills they could drip dirty water back down the window after you leave. I keep an assortment of different towels on me at all times.

Cleaning storefronts and restaurants is relatively easy. However, when you are inside of a restaurant. Make sure you arrive early in the morning several hours before the restaurant opens. make sure you are very clean and conscientious inside of the restaurant; especially when it comes to standing on booths and working around silverware plates, dust and things of that nature.

Whenever we clean restaurants, we always go back and wipe down the booth seats. *Trust me there are cases where you literally have no choice but to stand on the booth to clean the windows.*

Getting a microfiber ceiling fan attachment that goes on the end of your extension pole is an awesome way to make extra money. I charge $4 her ceiling fan and usually make an extra $16 to clean for ceiling fans in a restaurant. Make sure you show up early and move all silverware and plates off of the tables because dust will be falling everywhere.

Another option is to climb up the ladder with wet microfiber towels and physically clean the ceiling fans by hand. this I would charge $10 to $15 per fan and possibly $35 to $45 per fan if they're extremely high up. Carrying large, heavy, clunky ladders inside of a restaurant is a huge pain in the ass and most of the time not worth the extra couple bucks.

In the beginning, trust me you will do whatever it takes to make an extra couple bucks. But once you get your window cleaning business off the ground, Change your game up.

I try to avoid and stay away from any work that makes me dripping sweat for low pay. However, once your customer sees you climb on a ladder and do some crazy stuff.
Now he sees you as the "Guy who does the crazy stuff".

If you don't see this now, then you will see it in time. The more efficient you can make your business, the more money you make and the more you will begin to live the lifestyle that you we're hoping this business would bring you in the first place.

Obviously the best lifestyle business is where you've built an entire team of people who do the work for you while you sell jobs and collect checks. But for now it's time to bust a move.

Residential Homes

When you are in a residential home. My personal rule of thumb is that as soon as I walk into the door I go left and travel clockwise around the entire house. If there's stairs... leading upstairs...then I go up the stairs. If there are stairs leading down stairs, I go down the stairs. If there's a door leading into a room with windows, I go into that room.

I bet most window cleaners would disagree and say to do the first floor first, upstairs 2nd, basement third and garage windows last. but I'm really A.D.D. so I know for a fact that if no matter what I just keep going left, left, left clockwise no matter what. that I know for fact that I will not miss a single window.

There's also a couple different ways you can clean windows inside of a home.
Especially when you're doing "The Works Package". That includes window cleaning inside, outside, tracks scrubbed out, Sills wiped down plus screen cleaning.

It can take up to 12 minutes per window not including the screen.

if you're running around the house removing the screens and then cleaning just the glass and then scrubbing only the tracks and going back and wiping down the frames. That means you're wasting 80% of your time making repeated trips around the house just to return to the same damn window again and again. Very inefficient. m
More like avoidance behavior.

I prefer the one-and-done lean method. That's where you go ahead and clean everything that has to do with that specific window right then and there. So when you're done, you never have to touch that window again.

Whenever you're done cleaning a house. Keep your tool belt on because you should always do final walk-through and Quality Inspection. People are very smart. Especially Housewives. I have a ton of window cleaning clients and the Housewives are very particular.
They are not happy when they have to ask you to clean a window because it's dirty. however, they are very happy when they see diligently working to make sure that every window is perfect.

There are many ways to clean residential windows. Not saying that my way is the best way.
You just have to get out there and do it and learn the process for yourself.

Once again the average ranch house is about $149 bucks and the average 2 story Colonial home is about $200 bucks for all glass cleaned inside and out plus screen cleaning.

Please watch my YouTube videos. My channel is called the Window Cleaning Blueprint. Also own a landscaping company and have a ton of window cleaning videos on that channel too. the Landscaping Employee Trap on YouTube. go to playlist and select "window cleaning".

Your Window Cleaning Tool Belt

This doesn't have to be followed exactly by any means. It's just an example.
 hanging from your belt on every job should be

1.) Your filthy dirty wet microfiber towel for wiping down frames or scrubbing tracks
2.) Your damp Blue Surgical towel for wiping down window sills
3.) Your dry microfiber Powell 4 detailing the corners and drip lines of the window
4.) Your dry microfiber or surgical buffing towel 4 buffing out hazy spots on glass
5.) Your extra spare dry microfiber surgical buffing towel as a backup if the others get wet

A minimum of two squeegees. Preferably three or four.

1.) Your 22 inch Sorbo locking swivel T squeegee
2.) Your 16 inch Sorbo locking swivel T bar squeegee
3.) Your 12 inch Sorbo squeegee
4.) Your 8 inch baby squeegee for cleaning French panes and windows with mullions
5.) Your Unger Monsoon swivel t-bar microfiber scrubber (solution applicator)

6.) Your Unger Fixi-Clamp - "My favorite" it's a clamp that you stick a towel in to reach high.

7.) You're Ettore, Pulex or Ninja Sidekick "bucket on a belt" with holster.

8.) Possibly razor blades, *"only with proper education on window scratching issues"*

9.) Your Unger Velcro spray bottle holder, belt clip pouch

10.) Your Unger leather double squeegee holster. (Outdoors Only) Water Drips.

11.) Unger extension poles always

12.) An extra pair of blue plastic shoe cover booties

13.) A tough bristle monster head Duster for dusting screens

14.) A dry towel 4 dry cleaning screens

There's a million ways to do this

Truck or Van...Car?

When first getting started in the window cleaning business the world is your oyster.
I started out in a rusty 1991 Dodge Dakota truck called the Blue Goose.

Joshua Latimer Started out in a 1991 Cavalier with a ladder strapped to the top.
He's the same guy who ended up doing $100,000 a month and revenue cleaning windows before he sold his business and moved with his family to Costa Rica.

When you get the money comma a van is probably the most efficient tool for cleaning windows. But a truck with a cap on the back works well too. I currently have a pickup truck with a 12 by 6 foot enclosed trailer.

Once you get some decals, magnets or vinyl wrap your entire vehicle. You're on your way 2 launching and growing your own window cleaning business.

Chapter 19

Conclusion

No Matter What You Do Now. JUST GO!

One of my favorite sayings.
"Do not wait until you're good to get going. Get going and then you'll get good"

No matter what you do, just get started. I don't know your personal life story but I can almost guarantee it isn't an easy one.
 My uncle who is a small business owner told me something that I'll never forget.
 "As long as you work every inch of the day, you'll always make it".

I believe in you and I believe in your dreams. you can absolutely make $500 a day cleaning windows.
I know this may seem impossible right now. I felt the same way.
 To my amazement what I found, is that if you 100% commit yourself to learning the window cleaning business and stepping your game up.

You can absolutely make $500 a day and then some.

 I will conclude the book here.

WHAT'S NEXT

Now that you're equipped with all the basic tools and knowledge that you need to get your new window cleaning business off the ground. Or if you own an existing window cleaning business and want to make more money.
Here's what you do. Run! Run like your hair is on fire!
Go out there and make it happen. Go!

Go now and be great. I wish you the best of success my friend.

If you need more training I have an entire
Separately Sold video training course to go along with this book
http://www.TheWindowCleaningBlueprint .com

Sincerely,
Your friend in the battle.

Keith Kalfas.

P.S.

Lookout in the future for more books
And audio books from
Greenworld Publishing

I'm committed to lifelong achievement
and I hope you'll join me on the journey.

DISCLAIMER

The income and results disclosed in this program are not typical, but the people I talk about in this book are not typical either. Like any business, starting and growing a successful functional window cleaning business that makes a minimum $500 a day takes not only time, but an immense amount of hard work and sacrifice. Yes, my service make $500 a day and even more cleaning windows or I wouldn't have advertised this claim.

It's the truth that you too can make very good money cleaning windows. It's the truth that you must work your ass off and pay your dues. It's the truth that if you do not take your business seriously, carry yourself like a professional and learn marketing, business ethics, how to sell, have a great attitude, and act like a winner.

You probably won't make a penny in the window cleaning business, let alone anything related to being your own boss. If you can't learn how to develop the attitude of a winner and commit 100% to not only being a professional window cleaner. But a professional business person who carries proper licensing and insurance, practices safety, pays his taxes and is eager to learn in the face of challenge.
then The Window Cleaning Blueprint is not for you.
Upon consuming this program. I want to disclose that the window cleaning business is a very diverse and multi perspective business when it comes to what tools methods and prices one should use.
The water fed pole system is currently at it's pinnacle of window cleaning technology.
I do not claim to be an expert or authority about any of my claims in this program.
There are so many different ways to clean windows.
My way is probably not the best. So do not take my advice as gold.

Do your own research and find out what works best for you.
Now that I have stated my disclaimer.
I will not be held responsible at the helm of ridicule or scrutiny
by other professional window cleaners or professional window
cleaning associations
due to inaccurate information, or by you stating that my claims
are absolutely true.

The Window Cleaning Blueprint
How to Make $500 a Day Cleaning Windows

By Keith Kalfas

GreenWorld Publishing Copyright 2016

Find this and more titles from Greenworld Publishing
On Amazon Kindle and Audible.com.

Thank you for reading.
Now go and be great!

53729358R00091

Made in the USA
Lexington, KY
16 July 2016